A MICHIGAN Guide

Step Up to the TOEFL® iBT for Students at the Basic Level

NIGEL A. CAPLAN

Series Editor
LAWRENCE J. ZWIER

Ann Arbor
University of Michigan

ISBN-13: 978-0-472-03407-9

2013   2012   2011   2010   4   3   2   1

The test directions and sample questions printed in this book are not actual TOEFL® iBT test materials. Training materials and other testing information are provided in their entirety by the University of Michigan Press. No endorsement of this publication by Educational Testing Service should be inferred.

Series Preface

Success on the TOEFL® Internet-based Test (iBT) depends on skills that the iBT does not directly test. In particular, aspiring iBT candidates need practice with English grammar, vocabulary, and pronunciation. It is possible to practice these basics incidentally by working with typical iBT-preparation books, but only if you are already close to TOEFL® competence. Otherwise, the preparation books will simply be too hard. It's a circular problem: You can't practice the basics because you haven't got enough competence in the basics. The books in the University of Michigan Press's *Step Up* series are meant for students whose grammar, vocabulary, and pronunciation skills are not yet sufficient for full-scale TOEFL® preparation. As the title indicates, we are hoping to provide platforms from which a pre-TOEFL® student can work toward earnest preparation for the test.

Grammar instruction is at the foundation of *Step Up*, the platform on which vocabulary and pronunciation lessons are set. The selection of grammar points for each unit has been determined by functions commonly elicited on the iBT. For example, Unit 7 addresses the function of giving opinions. This is specifically tested in the writing and speaking sections of the iBT. It also often appears in reading and listening passages. In this book's Unit 7, then, we present relevant grammar (comparatives), vocabulary (opinion words), and pronunciation skills (word stress).

The *Step Up* series includes at least two volumes: basic and intermediate. They explain lexico-syntactic features of English that are taken to be understood in most other iBT-prep books. They offer practice in language points that, though basic, may not be firmly under control by students planning to take the test. This Basic volume addresses the texts and exercises appropriate for beginning-level students. The Intermediate volume is meant for students who are not too far from handling the English on the iBT but are not quite ready for it yet.

The vocabulary may seem at times a bit advanced. This is necessary and fitting for many reasons. As experienced teachers of English for Academic Purposes know very well, even grammatically shaky students can post significant gains in receptive vocabulary. Progress in this area helps ratchet forward the student's exposure to grammatically diverse discourse and serious, substantive texts like those on the iBT.

Seriousness and substance are constant attributes of the texts in the *Step Up* series. Just as philosophers since Cicero have noted that personal virtue entails gravitas—the ability to be taken seriously—so students look for a certain no-nonsense quality in TOEFL®-prep materials. This does not mean the practice passages are dour and inaccessible, but they can claim topical significance. The iBT content is academic, so the content in any TOEFL®-prep course should be as well.

This goes deeper than so-called face validity. Yes, tone is part of it. It is important for students to believe that even a basic-skills textbook treats them with respect; their motivation is likely to rest on that belief. The real test, however, is in whether students are more viable candidates for the iBT after using *Step Up*. We are confident they will be, and we hope you enjoy traveling with them in that direction.

—Lawrence J. Zwier, Series Editor

Acknowledgments

Grateful acknowledgment is given to the following individuals for lending their voices to the audio: Pat Grimes, Scott Ham, Joseph Jasina, Badria Jazairi, Alix Keener, and Sheryl Leicher.

I am, as always, grateful to Larry Zwier for his encouragement, insights, and feedback and to Kelly Sippell for her patience and editorial acumen. Thank you, too, to my wife, Ellisha, for letting me hibernate in the study to write, and to my son, Samuel, for sleeping through most of the process.

—N.A.C.

Contents

Scope and Sequence

Unit	Function	Vocabulary	Vocabulary Skill	Grammar	Speaking Clearly
1	Stepping up to the iBT	Words and phrases on the iBT	Keeping a vocabulary notebook	The Imperative Parts of speech	Syllables
2	Talking about yourself	Family Hobbies	Using flashcards	Simple present *Like/enjoy* + verb-*ing*	Vowel sounds: / ɪ / / i /
3	Describing people	Countries Feelings	Learning word families	Present progressive Negatives	Vowel sounds: / æ / / ay /
4	Describing places	Education Around town	Using a dictionary	Prepositions *If/When* sentences	Consonant sounds: / l / / r /
5	Describing your experiences	Strong verbs School words	Understanding roots	Simple past Irregular verbs	Pronouncing the *-ed* ending
6	Giving reasons	Likes and dislikes Service encounters	Understanding prefixes and suffixes	Asking questions Conjunctions	Consonant sounds: / š / / č / ž / / ǰ /
7	Giving opinions	Opinion words Adverbs	Guessing from context	Comparatives Modal verbs	Word stress
8	Summarizing	Sequence words Contrast words	Recognizing collocations	Superlatives Articles	Sentence stress

To the Teacher

Introduction

Step Up to the TOEFL® iBT for Students at the Basic Level, is a skills-based textbook that helps high-beginning/low-intermediate students prepare to take a **step up** toward the Test of English as a Foreign Language (TOEFL®). This is not a test-preparation book: instead, it teaches some of the fundamental **vocabulary, grammar, and pronunciation** skills necessary for the test. After completing the *Step Up* series, students should be ready to study a TOEFL®-level preparation book, such as *The Michigan Guide to English for Academic Success and Better TOEFL® Test Scores.*

The Internet-based TOEFL® (iBT) assumes a high level of linguistic competency, and many students may not have the language skills necessary to follow a test-preparation book or attempt the reading, writing, listening, and speaking tasks on the test. Therefore, *Step Up to the TOEFL® iBT* focuses on the underlying abilities that students need before they prepare to take the test. The *Basic Level* focuses on the building blocks for language competence: high-frequency vocabulary, essential grammatical structures, pronunciation of commonly confused sounds, basic stress patterns, and spelling. Although the TOEFL® does not directly score vocabulary, grammar, and pronunciation, weaknesses in these areas will severely impair students' performance on all areas of the test. Therefore, every point covered in *Step Up to the TOEFL® iBT* will benefit test-takers on one or more sections of the iBT.

Unit Tour

Each of the eight units addresses one rhetorical function and includes:

- **Learning Targets** and their relevance to the four sections of the test
- **Getting Started** questions to activate prior knowledge
- two **Vocabulary You Need** topics that introduce a range of key words used to accomplish the unit function, such as family vocabulary for Unit 2, Talking about Yourself
- a **Vocabulary Skill** to build learner autonomy in vocabulary acquisition
- two **Grammar You Can Use** topics that strengthen students' receptive and productive language
- samples of (near) test-level use of the grammar from *The Michigan Guide to English for Academic Success and Better TOEFL® Test Scores* and *Step Up to the TOEFL® iBT for Intermediate Students*

- a **Speaking Clearly** point focusing on basic pronunciation
- **Skill-Building Exercises** that practice the language point through high-interest reading, writing, listening, and speaking activities
- **iBT Practice Exercises** that give students practice in using the language point in tasks similar to ones on the actual test (including the integrated speaking and writing tasks) but at their level of competency
- **Step Up Notes** with useful hints and tips about stepping up to the TOEFL®
- **Word Boxes** for reading and listening exercises that gloss additional useful words
- a **Vocabulary Review** that lists all the new words in the unit; these words have been recorded and appear on the companion website (www.press.umich.edu/esl/compsite/stepup) for further pronunciation practice
- a **Spelling Skills** exercise that practices five key words from the unit.

Teaching Notes

Getting Started

The Getting Started questions encourage students to use the vocabulary, grammar, and pronunciation skills they already know to express the unit function. Here are some ways you can use these questions:

1. Ask students to write for five minutes on each question. Don't collect and grade the writing; use it as a fluency-building exercise.

2. Ask students to discuss the questions in pairs or small groups. With lower-level students, it is often helpful if they make some notes before they discuss. Then, conduct a whole-class discussion. This gives students two or three opportunities to express the same ideas.

 ### Vocabulary You Need

Each unit begins and ends with vocabulary, for it is by increasing the depth and breadth of vocabulary knowledge that students at this level can make the fastest progress in all skill areas. Vocabulary is presented in three ways:

- explicit instruction at the start of each unit
- implicit instruction through practice exercises
- supplementary vocabulary in Word Boxes for certain reading and listening exercises.

All the words are reviewed at the end of each unit. Here are some ways you can use the Vocabulary Review:

1. Ask students to listen and repeat to each word. Drill them on correct pronunciation.

2. Ask students to make entries in their vocabulary notebooks (see Vocabulary Skill in Unit 1, page 6).

3. Ask students to categorize the words, for example, by part of speech (nouns, verbs, adjectives, adverbs) or topic.

4. Quiz students on the words, using the review as a study tool.

5. Encourage students to use the new vocabulary by writing short paragraphs or dialogues.

6. Use the Spelling Skills exercise to focus attention on commonly confused sound/letter combinations. Remind students that no spell checker is available on the writing section of the iBT.

The primary focus in this book is on high-frequency content words from the General Service List (West 1953). However, a small number of commonly occurring words in university English from the Academic Word List (Coxhead 2000) have been included to help students step up toward academic English. Finally, many useful words for talking about higher education are included because the iBT places particular emphasis on them. A complete list of all the words covered in the book is provided in the Vocabulary Index; words on the General Service List and Academic Word List are marked.

Grammar You Can Use

Since the discrete grammar test has been removed from the TOEFL®, it is no longer useful to cram grammar rules and exceptions as a form of preparation for the test. However, it is also unrealistic for high-beginning/low-intermediate learners to study every possible grammar structure in English. Therefore, *Step Up to the TOEFL® iBT* focuses on grammar points that express the function of the unit and are fundamental to clear language use and basic comprehension. For example, the function in Unit 4 is Describing Places, and the grammar teaches prepositions (which are essential to give and understand directions) and *if/when* sentences, which are useful for geographical descriptions (for example, *When you come out of the library, turn left.*).

Here are some ways you can teach this section:

- Discuss the grammar presentation in class, and assign the exercises for homework or classwork.
- Have students attempt the first exercise in pairs, and evaluate their knowledge of the grammar point; they may only need the explanation for reference.
- Start with the test-level excerpt that you will find next to each grammar presentation; ask students to discuss the use of the words in bold.
- Divide students into pairs or small groups, and assign each group one grammar topic to present to the class.

The *Grammar You Can Use* sections do not provide the final word on these grammar points. Most areas of English grammar can be studied in increasing depth at higher levels (for example, Unit 4 only covers present real conditionals because they are frequent and useful; the intermediate level of *Step Up* covers unreal conditionals). For more comprehensive coverage of these and other grammar points, teachers may wish to consult a grammar textbook, such as Keith S. Folse's *Clear Grammar 1* (University of Michigan Press). The goal of *Step Up to the TOEFL® iBT* is to give students the confidence to understand these structures and use them accurately in order to step up to the next level of proficiency.

Speaking Clearly

This section focuses mainly on the features of pronunciation that will improve students' delivery scores on the speaking section of the iBT. The delivery score is affected by pace, fluency, pronunciation, and intonation. This basic-level book targets the most difficult sounds of English for many learners and introduces the concepts of syllables, word stress, and sentence stress.

Students can use the accompanying audio CD as a model to improve their fluency. If possible, it is beneficial for learners to record their voices using a computer, voice recorder, or cassette player. Teachers and students can then compare the recording to the models and easily see areas of strength and weakness. The sounds listed in Appendix A are included on the audio CD.

A Word about the Listening Exercises

Test-takers can listen to each lecture and conversation only once on the TOEFL®. In class or for self-study, learners studying this book are encouraged to listen more than once to most exercises for practice. However, to simulate the test conditions more closely, they can be restricted to one playback of the recording.

I hope you enjoy teaching *Step Up to the TOEFL® iBT for Students at the Basic Level,* and I wish your students good luck as they prepare for the test and their future studies!

—Nigel A. Caplan

References

Coxhead, A. "The New Academic Word List." *TESOL Quarterly,* *34,* no. 2 (2000): 213–38.

West, M. *A General Service List of English Words.* London: Longman, 1953.

To the Student

Have you already taken the Internet-based test (iBT)? Have you tried to read a TOEFL® preparation textbook? If so, you already know the language on the test is difficult. The readings and listenings are in an academic style. They discuss complex academic subjects. In order to answer the writing and speaking questions well, you need a lot of vocabulary, good grammar, and clear delivery.

Step Up to the TOEFL® iBT for Students at the Basic Level will help you take a **step up** toward the Test of English as a Foreign Language (TOEFL®). This is not a test-preparation book: instead, it teaches some of the **vocabulary, grammar, and pronunciation** skills you will need for the TOEFL®. After finishing this book and *Step Up to the TOEFL® iBT for Intermediate Students*, you should be ready to study a TOEFL®-preparation book such as *The Michigan Guide to English for Academic Success and Better TOEFL® Test Scores*.

In this book, you are going to learn a lot of vocabulary! These new words will help you improve your reading, writing, listening, and speaking skills. You will also study important grammar points. Your pronunciation will get better too, so people can understand you and you can understand them. There are no separate vocabulary, grammar, or pronunciation sections on the iBT, but you will need these skills to do well in all sections of the test.

Before you start *Step Up to the TOEFL® iBT: Basic Level*, look through a unit. You will see:

- the learning targets for the unit, and how they are useful for the iBT
- a Vocabulary Skill that you can use to learn vocabulary on your own
- examples of TOEFL®-level language in the grammar section; don't worry if you can't understand these yet
- a Vocabulary Review of all the new words from each unit
- a Spelling Skills practice exercise
- Step Up Notes with useful hints and tips for the TOEFL® iBT itself.

 On the audio CD, you will find all the listening exercises for each unit.

Good luck as you prepare to take the next **step up** toward the iBT and your future studies!

UNIT 1

Stepping Up to the iBT

Learning Targets	Importance on the iBT
Vocabulary —Words and phrases on the iBT —More words and phrases on the iBT *Vocabulary Skill:* Keeping a vocabulary notebook	• **iBT:** understand common words in directions and test questions (these words are also used in the exercises in *Step Up to the TOEFL® iBT*)
Grammar —The imperative —Parts of speech	• **iBT:** understand test questions written in the imperative (command) form • **iBT Writing and Speaking:** improve accuracy scores by using parts of speech correctly
Speaking Clearly —Syllables	• **iBT Speaking:** recognize and produce the correct number of syllables for clear, accurate pronunciation • **iBT Listening:** count syllables correctly to recognize and understand words and parts of speech

Getting Started

Discuss these questions.

1. What do you know about the TOEFL® iBT?

2. How do you study for a test?

Vocabulary You Need

I. Words and Phrases on the iBT

Read this description of the Internet-based TOEFL® Test (iBT):

> The iBT has four **sections.** Read the **directions** carefully!
>
> 1. **Reading:** Read three **passages,** and **choose** the **correct answer choice** for each question.
>
> 2. **Listening**: Listen to **lectures** and **conversations.** Answer questions **based on the information** in the lectures and conversations. Sometimes, you listen again to a short passage.
>
> 3. **Speaking:** There are **independent tasks** and **integrated tasks.** In the independent tasks, you talk about yourself. In the integrated tasks, you talk about a listening or reading passage.
>
> 4. **Writing:** There are integrated tasks and independent tasks. In the integrated tasks, you **match** the **essential** information from a reading with a listening. In the independent tasks, you write about your **opinion.**

Exercise 1.1

Fill the blanks with a bold word from the box. The first one has been done for you as an example.

1. Each part of the iBT is called a __section_____.

2. The instructions for a test are called the _____.

3. In the reading section, you read three _____ (for example, a paragraph from a textbook or an email).

4. An _____ task uses reading or listening with speaking or writing.

5. The independent writing task asks for your _____ about something.

iBT

EXERCISE 1.2

Read the test directions. Then, choose the correct answer for each question.

Test Directions

Complete the sentences with the best word.

1. What do you have to do?
   a. write sentences
   b. finish sentences
   c. listen to sentences

The speaker talks about which of **the following**?
   ❑ music
   ❑ art
   ❑ writing

2. What does "the following" mean here?
   a. the three answer choices
   b. the next question
   c. the students

Listen to the lecture. You can **take notes**.

3. What can you do?
   a. talk about the lecture
   b. ask questions
   c. write words from the lecture

Put a **check** in the correct place.

4. What do you write?
   a. X
   b. ✓
   c. *

Match the **appropriate** sentences with the topic they describe.

5. What does "appropriate" mean here?
   a. correct
   b. incorrect
   c. interesting

Exercise 1.3

Track 2. Listen to the conversations. Choose the correct answer to complete the sentences.

1. The students are starting the reading _____ of the test.

    a. passage

    b. section

    c. questions

2. This listening passage is a _____.

    a. conversation

    b. lecture

    c. test

3. This describes an _____ task.

    a. independent

    b. integrated

    c. interesting

4. How many times do the students listen to the passage?

    a. 0

    b. 1

    c. 2

5. What can the students do?

    a. Take notes.

    b. Write on the test paper.

    c. Talk about the lecture.

> *Step Up Note: Many questions on the reading and listening sections of the iBT ask you about details, so pay attention!*

II. More Words and Phrases on the iBT

Here are some words and phrases that you will see in iBT tasks and in this book.

What is the **main idea** of the passage?

What does the **author** say about books?

Why does the professor **mention** television?

Why does the man **hold this opinion?**

What is the lecture **mainly** about?

What **topics** do the students **discuss?**

Give **specific** details in your answer.

According to the woman, why are computers useful?

Do you **agree** or **disagree** with the following **statement?**

Describe the problem.

The author **discusses** football as an **example** of which of the following?

The word *quiz* in the passage is **closest** in meaning to:

Exercise 1.4

Choose bold words from the box that match the definitions. The first one has been done for you as an example.

1. most similar   <u>closest</u>

2. mostly   _____

3. talk about   _____, _____, _____

4. precise, exact   _____

5. in the words of   _____

6. have   _____

7. writer   _____

8. subjects   _____

Exercise 1.5

Match the test vocabulary on the left with the appropriate word(s) on the right. Use a dictionary to help you. The first one has been done for you as an example.

1. _c_ **Summarize** the lecture.

2. ____ **Explain** the meaning of *appropriate*.

3. ____ **Identify** the problem.

4. ____ **Include** specific examples in your answer.

5. ____ What **point** does the author make?

6. ____ What does this **quotation** from the passage mean?

a. say what something means

b. give or add

c̸. write or say the main ideas

d. idea

e. find and name

f. exact words of the author

Vocabulary Skill: Keeping a Vocabulary Notebook

You need to learn a lot of vocabulary to succeed on the TOEFL® iBT. A good way to help you keep and remember vocabulary is to use a vocabulary notebook. Take a new notebook (or use your computer), and write all the new words you learn. Include as much information about each word as possible, for example:

- spelling
- pronunciation
- noun, verb, or adjective
- definition
- translation
- example sentence
- similar words

Here is an example of an entry from a vocabulary notebook:

lecture (noun) / lɛkčər /
a talk by a professor at a university
Example: Today's lecture is about the business of sports.
Similar words: talk, class

Grammar You Can Use

I. The Imperative

> **Describe** the problem.
> **Summarize** the lecture.
> **Match** the words to the definitions.
> **Explain** the author's main point.

The verbs in the box (the words in **bold**) are **imperatives**, or commands. They give directions. Imperatives are very common in test questions and textbooks. The imperative is the base form of the verb. You do not use a subject (*you, he, the students*) with an imperative.

 The Next Step

- To tell someone NOT to do something (**a negative imperative**), use *don't* or *do not* before the verb (for example, *Don't write on the test booklet.*).
- It is polite to say *please* when you use an imperative in conversation.

---

iBT

EXERCISE 1.6

Track 3. Listen to the professor giving directions for a test. You can take notes. Place a check (✓) next to each of the professor's directions.

1. _____ Choose one section: grammar or writing.

2. _____ Answer all the questions.

3. _____ Write in pencil.

4. _____ Choose one answer choice for each question.

5. _____ Write two answers in the writing section.

6. _____ Give specific details and examples.

Exercise 1.7

Complete each sentence with a different verb from the box. Use the imperative. The first one has been done for you as an example.

explain	choose	ask	~~identify~~	summarize	include

1. _____Identify_____ the student's problem.

2. _____ the appropriate answer for each question.

3. _____ the reading passage is 100–120 words.

4. _____ the meaning of the word *integrated*.

5. _____ two examples in your answer.

6. _____ me questions at any time.

Exercise 1.8

Describe the iBT to a friend. Your friend does not know the test. Use imperatives (for example, Complete all four sections.). Use the information in the box on page 2 to help you. Talk for about 30 seconds; record your answer if possible.

II. Parts of Speech

Each word in an English sentence works as a part of speech. Some words have similar forms in different parts of speech, and some words have different forms in different parts of speech. Look at the pairs of sentences.

1. a. Listen to the **lecture**.	*lecture* is a **noun**.
b. The professor **lectures** for one hour.	*lectures* is a **verb**.
2. a. What is the **main** idea?	*main* is an **adjective**.
b. The passage is **mainly** about fish.	*mainly* is an **adverb**.

Here is a summary of the main parts of speech.

Part of Speech	Examples	Explanation
Noun	*lecture, topic, class, test*	names things, people, or ideas
Verb	*explain, identify, is, have, do*	shows actions or states
Adjective	*main, important, correct*	describes nouns
Adverb	*mainly, slowly, unfortunately*	gives information about verbs, adjectives, and sentences
Article	*a, an, the*	used with some nouns
Preposition	*on, in, at, under, near*	describes place, time, or position

There are many types of verbs. Two important types are **main verbs** (for example, *say, discuss, write, choose*) and **helping verbs** (for example, *is* in *He is talking*; *doesn't* in *She doesn't like it*; and *have* in *I have traveled to China*).

Exercise 1.9

Identify the part of speech of the <u>underlined</u> word. Choose from the words in the box. The first one has been done for you as an example.

~~noun~~   main verb   helping verb   adjective   adverb

1. The <u>test</u> is in four sections.   _____noun_____

2. The author <u>writes</u> about chocolate.   _____

3. This is an <u>exciting</u> book!   _____

4. What <u>does</u> this word mean?   _____

5. You speak so <u>quickly</u>!   _____

Exercise 1.10

Choose the correct word to complete each sentence. The first one has been done for you as an example.

1. This is a good (explain / (explanation) / explaining) of the passage.

2. The (main / mainly) idea of the lecture is the importance of healthy eating.

3. I'm writing a (summary / summarize / summarizing) of today's class.

4. My professor is the (write / writer / writing) of our textbook.

5. Answer every question (complete / completely).

Speaking Clearly

Syllables

A **syllable** is a unit of sound. A word can have one syllable, or it can have many syllables. Recognizing and producing the correct number of syllables will help people understand you better. Look at to the number of syllables in the words in the chart.

Word	Number of Syllables	Pronunciation*
test	1	/ tɛst /
answer	2	/ æn-sər /
direction	3	/ də-rɛk-šən /

Exercise 1.11

Track 4. Listen to the words. Write the number of syllables in each word. The first one has been done for you as an example.

1. section   __2__   5. explain   _____

2. task   _____   6. opinion   _____

3. question   _____   7. topic   _____

4. identify   _____   8. notes   _____

Practice saying the words with the correct number of syllables.

---

* These are **phonetic symbols,** which help you to "read" pronunciation. See Appendix A for a complete list of the phonetic symbols used in this book.

Step Up Note: The paragraph in Exercise 1.12 is similar to an answer to an independent speaking question on the iBT.

iBT

EXERCISE 1.12

Track 5. Listen to the paragraph. Then complete the paragraph by choosing the word you hear. Use the number of syllables you hear to help you.

How do you study for a test?

I always ① (study / studying) the directions for the test first. Then, I

② (main / mainly) review my notes and ③ (write / writer) practice essays.

I ask my teacher to ④ (explain / explanation) difficult points. I also like

⑤ (describe / describing) the test to a friend. If I can do that, I'm sure I

understand everything!

Read the paragraph as you listen to the audio CD. Listen for the number of syllables in each word.

Vocabulary Review

Review the vocabulary from Unit 1. Write new words in your vocabulary notebook. You can listen to them on the book's companion website.

according to	disagree	mention
adjective	discuss	noun
adverb	essential	opinion
again	explain	part of speech
agree	following	passage
answer choice	helping verb	point
appropriate	hold an opinion	preposition
article	identify	quotation
author	include	reading
based on	incorrect	section
checkmark	independent	speaking
choose	information	specific
closest	integrated	statement
complete	lecture	summary
conversation	listening	syllable
correct	main idea	take notes
describe	main verb	tasks
details	mainly	topic
directions	match	writing

Spelling Skills

Write the correct letters in the words from Unit 1.

1. There are four se____ ____ ions on the iBT.

2. Compl____ ____ ____ the sentences with the correct words.

3. Please give an e ____ ____ ____ ple.

4. It is essen____ ____ ____ ____ to read the questions carefully.

5. Having a convers ____ ____ ____ ____ n in English is a good way to practice for the test.

UNIT 2

Talking about Yourself

Learning Targets	Importance on the iBT
Vocabulary —Family —Hobbies *Vocabulary Skill:* Using flashcards	• **iBT Reading and Listening:** understand passages on social science topics • **iBT Speaking:** describe personal experiences and familiar topics • **iBT Independent Writing:** answer personal experience questions
Grammar —The simple present tense —*Like/enjoy* + verb-*ing*	• **iBT Reading and Listening:** understand the meaning of the simple present, the most common tense in academic English • **iBT Writing and Speaking:** use basic grammar correctly for improved accuracy
Speaking Clearly —Vowel sounds / ɪ / and / i /	• **iBT Speaking:** pronounce vowel sounds correctly for better delivery • **iBT Listening:** recognize words by identifying the correct vowel sound

Getting Started

Discuss these questions.

1. How many people are in your family? Talk or write about them.

2. What are your hobbies?

Vocabulary You Need

I. Family

*Study the **family tree** with words for members of a family.*

great grandmother = great grandfather
|
grandmother = grandfather

aunt = uncle   **mother = father**

cousin   **brother**   **YOU**   **sister = brother-in-law**

niece   **nephew**

Here are other words and phrases to talk about the family.

parents	mother + father
grandparents	grandmother + grandfather
children	sons + daughters
sibling	brother or sister
only child	having no brothers or sisters
married	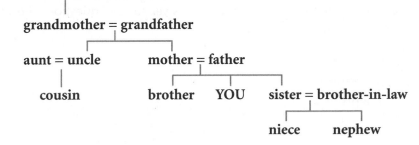
divorced	
stepmother	Your father's wife, but not your mother

Exercise 2.1

Complete the sentences with bold words from the family tree. The first one has been done for you as an example.

1. Your mother's sister is your __aunt_____.

2. Your father's father is your _____.

3. Your sister's husband is your _____.

4. Your aunt's children are your _____.

5. Your grandmother's father is your _____.

Step Up Note: *Not all of the listening passages on the iBT are lectures. You will also hear conversations like the one in Exercise 2.2.*

EXERCISE 2.2

Track 6. Listen to the conversation between a student and her professor. You can take notes. Choose the correct answer to each question. The first one has been done for you as an example.

1. Who is the woman?
   a. a student
   b. a professor
   c. Frank

2. What class does the professor teach?
   a. math
   b. chemistry
   c. English

3. Is this Julie's first class with this professor?
   a. yes
   b. no
   c. The passage doesn't say.

4. Who does the professor know in Julie's family?
   a. her sister
   b. her brother
   c. her nephew

5. What do you know about Julie's brother, Frank?
   a. He's married.
   b. He's divorced.
   c. He's a student.

6. How many children does Frank have?
   a. 0
   b. 1
   c. 2

Exercise 2.3

1. *Draw your family tree. Start with yourself. Use the family tree on page 15 as a model.*

2. *Describe your family tree. Talk for about 45 seconds; record your answer if possible.*

II. Hobbies

Here are some hobbies.

a. playing sports

b. swimming

c. watching movies

d. reading

e. gardening

f. playing the
piano

g. painting

h. playing video
games

Here are some words and phrases to talk about your hobbies.

> Playing sports is **fun**.
>
> Video games are **exciting**.
>
> I like reading in my **spare time.**
>
> I **enjoy** watching movies.
>
> Painting is **relaxing**.

 ### Exercise 2.4

Do you enjoy these hobbies? Place a check (✓) in the Yes or No column. Use a dictionary to help you understand any new words. Share your answers with a partner.

Hobby	Yes	No
1. knitting		
2. riding horses		
3. taking photographs		
4. hiking		
5. bird watching		
6. singing		
7. playing board games		
8. scrap-booking		

iBT

Exercise 2.5

Read the passage about a hobby called *letterboxing*. People who do this hobby are called *letterboxers*.

Letterboxing is an old hobby, but it is now popular again. People hide plastic boxes in secret places. They write a clue and post it on the Internet. Letterboxers solve the clue and go hiking to find the box. Inside the box, there is a book and a stamp. Letterboxers use the stamp to show they found the box. Letterboxing is fun and exciting for children and adults.

clue = something that helps you solve a problem
stamp = a tool for printing a shape on paper

Choose the correct answer to each question.

1. Which of these sentences about letterboxing is true?
    a. Nobody goes letterboxing today.
    b. Letterboxing is a new hobby.
    c. Letterboxing is a popular old hobby.

2. What is a *letterbox*?
    a. a person
    b. a box
    c. a hobby

Step Up Note: The word except *makes a question negative. The correct answer is the only one that is NOT true. Negative questions like this are common on the reading section of the test.*

3. Letterboxers do all of the following EXCEPT
    a. use the Internet
    b. go hiking
    c. take photographs

4. Who enjoys letterboxing?
    a. children
    b. parents
    c. children and adults

5. The word *post* in the reading means
    a. send
    b. write about
    c. draw

Exercise 2.6

Complete the sentences about your hobbies using words from this unit.

1. My favorite hobby is _____.

2. I like it because it is _____.

3. I also enjoy _____.

4. I like _____ in my spare time.

Step Up Note: *Practice typing your answers on an English keyboard. You have to type your essays on the writing section when you take the iBT.*

Vocabulary Skill: Using Flashcards

Your vocabulary notebook helps you to collect words. You also need to test yourself on new words. Flashcards are a convenient way to do this. A flashcard is a small card. Write the vocabulary word on one side. On the other side of the card, write the meaning and an example sentence.

hobby (noun)	free time activity My hobby is swimming.

You can use the cards to test yourself. Put the cards in a pile. Look at the word on the card. Read the word. Say the meaning. Now, turn the card over. Check your answer. Or, look at the meaning, and say the word. Check your answer. If you get the correct answer, put the card away. If not, put the card to the back and test yourself again later.

Grammar You Can Use

I. The Simple Present Tense

All the verbs in the two sentences in the quotation are in the **simple present tense**. The simple present tense means that the action or state *always* or *usually* happens. Use the simple present to describe facts and things that do not change. To form the simple present tense, follow the rules.

> "Babies' first contact **is** with their parents. For example, they **learn** to smile by copying their parents. As a result, children **learn** their social behavior from them."
>
> —*Step Up to the TOEFL" iBT for Intermediate Students, p. 36*

- After *he, she, it,* or a **singular noun** (for example, *hobby, sister, family*), add **-s** to the verb (for example, *my brother swims*).
- If the verb ends in **-ch** or **-sh**, add **-es** (for example, *he teaches, she washes*).

Exercise 2.7

Complete the sentences with the correct form of the verb in parentheses. Look up any new words in your dictionary, and write them in your vocabulary notebook. The first one has been done for you as an example.

1. (like)   My sister _likes_____ knitting.

2. (play)   Many teenagers _____ video games.

3. (teach)   My father _____ at the high school.

4. (get)   Some people _____ married when they are 18 years old.

5. (watch)   I always _____ TV on weekends.

Exercise 2.8

Track 7. Listen to the lecture about children and sports. You can take notes. Use your notes to choose the correct answer to the questions.

> *physical education* = sports classes at school
> *healthy* = good for your body
> *put on weight* = to get heavier

1. Why do schools sometimes stop physical education classes?

   a. to make money

   b. to save money

   c. to teach children

2. The speaker mentions that sports are important for children for all of the following reasons EXCEPT

   a. Playing sports is good for your health.

   b. Sports build team skills.

   c. Sports improve grades.

3. What can happen to children without sports at school?

   a. They can put on weight.

   b. They can save money.

   c. They can be healthier.

4. Who do you think the speaker is?

   a. a student

   b. a professor

   c. a soccer player

Exercise 2.9

Track 8. Listen again to four sentences from the lecture in Exercise 2.8. Complete the sentences with simple present verbs.

1. The topic of today's lecture _____ physical education in schools.

2. Schools sometimes _____ physical education classes to save money.

3. Sports _____ important for children.

4. Children _____ a hobby.

II. *Like/enjoy* + Verb-*ing*

The verbs *like* and *enjoy* are sometimes followed by verb-*ing*. For example, we say, *I **like watching** movies on DVD.* Some other verbs in this pattern are: *enjoy, prefer, love, hate,* and *dislike.*

> "The student prefers **raising** more money by increasing the costs. She favors **raising** more money because she thinks the university's cost is very low."
>
> —adapted from *The Michigan Guide to English for Academic Success and Better TOEFL® Test Scores,* p. 198

Exercise 2.10

*Read this passage. <u>Underline</u> all the **verb-*ing*** forms. The first one has been done for you as an example.*

Some people prefer <u>having</u> a large family. For example, my friend has five siblings. She loves being with them. She enjoys spending the holidays with all her family. Other people like being in a small family. I am an only child. I like spending time alone, but I also enjoy spending time with my friend's large family. Overall, I prefer my small family, but I like having a lot of friends!

spending (the holidays / time with) = passing time in a certain way

EXERCISE 2.11

Track 9. Listen to the passage in Exercise 2.10. This could be an answer to an independent speaking task on the iBT. The question is: **Do you agree or disagree with this statement?** *It is better to have a large family than a small family.*

Choose the correct answer to each question.

1. Does the speaker prefer having a large or small family?

   a. He prefers having a large family.

   b. He prefers having a small family.

   c. He does not say.

2. Why does he talk about his friend?

   a. She prefers having a small family.

   b. She is an only child.

   c. She has five siblings.

3. Why does his friend like having a large family?

   a. She enjoys spending time with her siblings.

   b. She enjoys playing with her siblings.

   c. She goes swimming with her siblings.

4. How many siblings does the speaker have?
   a. 0
   b. 1
   c. 5

5. What does the speaker say about having friends?
   a. Friends are better than siblings.
   b. He does not have many friends.
   c. He likes having many friends.

iBT

EXERCISE 2.12

Do you agree or disagree with this statement? *It is better to have a large family than a small family.* Prepare to talk about this question. Write the information you will need.

1. Do you prefer having a large or small family? _____

2. Write one or two reasons for your answer.

    _____

    _____

3. Give one or two examples.

    _____

    _____

4. Use your answers to 1, 2, and 3 to speak about the question. Talk for about 45 seconds; record your answer if possible.

Step Up Note: On the speaking section of the iBT, you will have 15 seconds to prepare and 45 seconds to speak on a question like this one. You won't have time to write full sentences on your note paper.

Speaking Clearly

Vowel Sounds: / ɪ / and / i /

The sounds / ɪ / and / i / are very different in English. You hear the / ɪ / sound in words like _is_, _swimming_, and _sister_. You hear the / i / sound in words like _read_, _nearby_, and _keep_. Sometimes the sound can change the meaning of the word—for example, _ship_ and _sheep_.

Exercise 2.13

Track 10. Listen to the words. Place a check (✓) in the correct column for the underlined sound. The first one has been done for you as an example.

	/ ɪ /	/ i /
1. sp**ea**k		✓
2. m**e**		
3. fam**i**ly		
4. famil**y**		
5. b**ea**ch		
6. marr**ie**d		
7. d**i**vorced		
8. s**i**bling		

Practice reading the words correctly.

Exercise 2.14

Track 11. Listen to the words. Place a check (✓) next to the word you hear. The first one has been done for you as an example.

1. a. [   ] it   b. [✔] eat

2. a. [   ] ship   b. [   ] sheep

3. a. [   ] this   b. [   ] these

4. a. [   ] hill   b. [   ] heel

5. a. [   ] pill   b. [   ] peel

Repeat the exercise with a partner. Take turns saying one word from each pair (for example, eat). Your partner checks the word he or she hears.

EXERCISE 2.15

Answer the questions. Talk for 30 seconds about each question. Try to pronounce / I / and / i / correctly. Talk to a partner, or record your answers.

1. Who is your favorite family member? Talk about him or her.

2. What is your favorite hobby, and why?

3. Are sports important for young people? Why?

Vocabulary Review

Review the vocabulary from Unit 2. Write new words in your vocabulary notebook. You can listen to them on the book's companion website.

aunt	grandparents	playing the piano
bird watching	great grandfather	playing video games
board games	great grandmother	prefer
brother	hate	put on weight
brother-in-law	healthy	relaxing
children	hiking	riding horses
clue	hobby	scrap-booking
cousin	knitting	sibling
dislike	love	singing
divorced	married	sister
enjoy	mother	spare time
exciting	nephew	stamp
family tree	niece	stepmother
father	only child	surfing the Internet
fun	painting	swimming
gardening	parents	taking photographs
grandfather	physical education	uncle
grandmother	playing sports	watching movies

abc Spelling Skills

Correct the spelling mistakes in the words from Unit 2.

1. grandmohter   _____

2. swiming   _____

3. vidoe games   _____

4. put on weiht   _____

5. hobbie   _____

UNIT 3

Describing People

Learning Targets	Importance on the iBT
Vocabulary —Countries —Feelings *Vocabulary Skill:* Learning word families	• **iBT Reading and Listening:** understand history and geography texts with place names • **iBT Independent Speaking and Writing:** give examples from your home culture; describe experiences involving people you know • **iBT Listening:** recognize speakers' emotions to answer the "attitude" questions
Grammar —The present progressive tense —Negatives	• **iBT Speaking and Listening:** understand and use the present progressive, an important tense in spoken English • **iBT Reading:** identify negatives to understand facts; answer questions that include negative words
Speaking Clearly —Vowel sounds / æ / and / ay /	• **iBT Speaking:** pronounce vowel sounds correctly for better delivery • **iBT Listening:** recognize words by identifying the correct vowel sound

Getting Started

Discuss these questions.

1. Where are you from? Do you have friends from other countries? Where are they from?

2. Describe a person you know well.

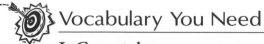

Vocabulary You Need

I. Countries

When you learn words for countries, also learn the adjectives.

Min is from **China**. She's **Chinese.**
Jin is from **Korea**. He's **Korean.**
Maria is from **Mexico.** She's studying at a **Mexican** university.
France, Germany, and **Italy** are in **Europe**. They're **European** countries.
John is from **the U.S.** He's an **American** citizen.

Exercise 3.1

Track 12. Listen to the conversations, and complete the sentences.

accent = regional pronunciation *nineteenth century* = 1800s *lunar* = about the moon

1. Michael is _____.

2. Their teacher is from _____.

3. Many people came to America from _____.

4. The man is wearing a _____ shirt.

5. Today is a holiday in many countries in _____.

iBT

EXERCISE 3.2

Read the passage about the United Kingdom.

The United Kingdom (U.K.) is really called the United Kingdom of Great Britain and Northern Ireland. Great Britain is, in fact, three countries: England, Scotland, and Wales. People from Scotland are Scottish and British. They don't like being called English! Many people from other countries live in the U.K. You can meet Indian, Chinese, Polish, and South African people in many British cities.

Choose the correct answer to each question.

1. Which of these countries is in the U.K.?
   a. Ireland
   b. Northern Ireland
   c. France

2. How many countries are in Great Britain?
   a. one
   b. three
   c. four

3. People from Scotland like being called all of the following EXCEPT
   a. British
   b. Scottish
   c. English

4. Which of these statements is true, according to the passage?
   a. There are not many Welsh people in the U.K.
   b. There are only English people in Britain.
   c. There are people from many countries in the U.K.

5. Which people are NOT mentioned in the passage?
   a. Polish
   b. Chinese
   c. French

Exercise 3.3

Answer two of the questions. Talk to a friend, or record your answers.

1. Where is your family from? Have they always lived in the same country?

2. What countries do you like visiting? Why?

3. Are you going to another country soon? Where?

II. Feelings

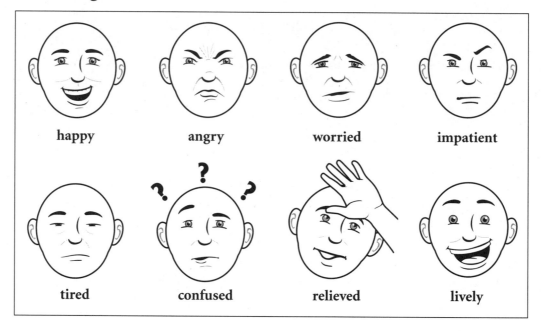

happy   angry   worried   impatient

tired   confused   relieved   lively

You can use sentences like these to describe feelings:

She **is** angry.

He **has** a nice **personality.**

I **am feeling** tired.

Exercise 3.4

Complete the sentences using words from the box on page 32.

1. My computer isn't working again. I hate it! I'm so _____.

2. Do you understand? You look _____.

3. She always has a lot of energy. She has a _____ personality.

4. I'm waiting for my test results. I'm really _____.

5. I worked so hard on my homework. I'm _____ now that it's finished.

Step Up Note: Some questions on the listening section of the iBT ask you to describe the speaker's attitude or opinion. You can answer these questions by recognizing the speaker's feelings and emotions.

EXERCISE 3.5

Track 13. Read the words in the box. Look up any new words in a dictionary. Then, listen to the speakers. Write the correct feeling for each person.

sad	enthusiastic	relieved	confident	nervous

1. _____

2. _____

3. _____

4. _____

5. _____

EXERCISE 3.6

Answer the questions. Talk to a friend, or record your answers.

1. Describe a friend who has a different personality from yours.

2. Do you have a favorite teacher? Describe him or her.

Vocabulary Skill: Learning Word Families

Many words in English are part of a *family*—related words with different parts of speech. Learning the members of a word family can quickly increase your vocabulary. (A dash means the word doesn't take that form.)

Noun	Verb	Adjective	Adverb
description	describe	descriptive	descriptively
America an American	——	American	——
enthusiasm	——	enthusiastic	enthusiastically

Grammar You Can Use

I. The Present Progressive Tense

The **present progressive tense** describes actions and feelings that are happening now. It has two parts: the helping verb *be* and the main verb-*ing*.

> "**I'm taking** Econ 120 this semester, and **I'm looking for** the textbook."
>
> —*Step Up to the TOEFL® iBT for Intermediate Students*, p. 3

> I **am feeling** sick.
>
> He **is studying** in the U.S.
>
> My TV **isn't working.**

Don't use the present progressive for things that are **always** true. Use the simple present.

> He **has** a lively personality.
> They **are** European.

Watch Your Step!

- In speaking and informal writing, the *be* verb is often made shorter: *I'm feeling. He's studying. They're working.*

Step Up Note: *You may read a university announcement as part of an integrated speaking task on the iBT.*

EXERCISE 3.7

Read the announcement, and <u>underline</u> the present progressive verbs.

> Professor Foote is feeling sick today, so he is staying at home. Today's class is canceled. However, a discussion is happening online. Please go to the class website, and write your opinion about today's readings.

canceled = not happening
online = on the Internet; on a website

Choose the correct answer to each question.

1. Why is today's class cancelled?
   a. The class is online.
   b. The professor is feeling sick.
   c. The students are staying at home.

2. Does Professor Foote always stay at home?
   a. yes
   b. no
   c. The passage doesn't say.

3. What are the students doing today?
   a. They are discussing the readings online.
   b. They are reading the textbook.
   c. They are waiting for the professor.

4. When is today's assignment due?
   a. tomorrow
   b. next week
   c. The passage doesn't say.

Exercise 3.8

Complete the sentences with the correct form of the verb in parentheses. Use the simple present or present progressive tense. The first one has been done for you as an example.

1. (listen)   Be quiet! I ____am listening____ to the news.

2. (wear)   She _____ a beautiful dress today.

3. (like)   I _____ listening to music.

4. (move)   This class _____ to room 101 for today only.

5. (talk)   The student _____ to her teaching assistant.

EXERCISE 3.9

Track 14. Listen to the conversation between a student and the teaching assistant. You can take notes. Use your notes to choose the correct answer to each question.

> *due on* = must be ready on this day
> *turn in* = to give homework to a teacher

1. Who is the woman?
   a. a student
   b. a teaching assistant
   c. a professor

2. How is the man feeling?
   a. worried
   b. happy
   c. relieved

3. What does the woman say about the student's grade?
   a. He always gets a good grade.
   b. She does not know his grade.
   c. He is getting a good grade in this class.

4. What is the man's problem?
   a. He does not like taking the class.
   b. He is taking five classes.
   c. He is failing this class.

5. What is the woman's reaction to his problem?

   a. It is a common problem.

   b. Only the student has this problem.

   c. She has the same problem.

6. Why does the woman NOT give the man a decision?

   a. She does not make decisions about due dates.

   b. She is not making decisions about this class.

   c. She is worried about her decision.

Exercise 3.10

Look for pictures in magazines or online. Find a picture or photograph of people. Describe the picture. What are the people doing? What are they feeling? What are they wearing? What is happening? Talk to a partner, or record your answer. Use the present progressive tense.

II. Negatives

When you are reading and listening, pay attention to **negative words**. Test questions on the iBT can ask you to choose an answer that is *not* correct. You can also use negative words to improve your language on the speaking and writing sections. Here are some negative words.

> "Arguing is **never** a good solution to a conflict. **No one** benefits from an argument that does **not** resolve the fundamental problem."
>
> —possible passage from an iBT integrated task

not	never	none	no one
no	not . . . any	nothing	nowhere

Watch Your Step!

- We often say and write *n't* for *not*: He **isn't** happy. The problems **aren't** easy to solve.

Exercise 3.11

Underline all the negative words in the paragraph.

Is there a Loch Ness Monster? No one knows the answer to this question. There is not any evidence for the monster, but this does not mean that there is nothing in the lake. There are many attempts every year to find the monster, but none is ever successful. Is the monster hiding? Or is it just a legend? We may never know for certain.

> *monster* = a horrible animal
> *evidence* = proof, things you can see
> *legend* = a story that is not true

EXERCISE 3.12

Track 15. Listen to the lecture about electric cars (cars that use electricity, not gasoline). You can take notes.

> *battery* = something that stores electricity
> *attractive* = having a quality that people want
> *pollution* = something that makes the environment dirty

According to the lecture, is the following information true or false? Place a check (✓) in the correct column.

	True	False
1. You can buy an electric car today.		
2. There are good batteries for electric cars.		
3. Today's electric cars don't drive far.		
4. There is no air pollution from making electricity.		
5. Electric cars are better for the environment than normal cars.		

EXERCISE 3.13

Disagree with the statements. Use a negative sentence for each answer. Write your answer, and then practice speaking it. The first one has been done for you as an example, but write your own answer to this question.

1. Electric cars are a good form of transportation.

   Electric cars are not a good form of transportation. There aren't any

   batteries, and they don't use clean energy.

   Your answer: _____

   _____

2. School uniforms are good for education.

   _____

   _____

3. Middle school students need cell phones.

   _____

   _____

4. Music makes people feel relaxed.

   _____

   _____

5. Vocabulary tests are important for students.

   _____

   _____

Step Up Note: In the speaking and writing sections of the iBT, you can agree or disagree with some of the ideas.

Speaking Clearly

Vowel Sounds: / æ / and / ay /

Be careful with the vowel sounds / æ / as in *rat* and / ay / as in *right*. The / ay / sound has two parts, / a / and / y /, to make / ay /.

Exercise 3.14

Track 16. Listen to the words. Place a check (✓) in the correct column for the underlined sound.

	/ æ /	/ ay /
1. Fr<u>a</u>nce		
2. Ch<u>i</u>na		
3. <u>a</u>ccent		
4. onl<u>i</u>ne		
5. rel<u>a</u>xed		
6. l<u>i</u>vely		
7. t<u>i</u>red		
8. <u>a</u>nswer		
9. n<u>i</u>ne		
10. descr<u>i</u>be		

Step Up Note: *The paragraph in Exercise 3.15 is similar to an answer you might give on an independent speaking task on the iBT.*

iBT

EXERCISE 3.15

Track 17. Listen to the paragraph. Complete the paragraph with the words you hear.

Describe a friend who is very different from you.

I am going to ① _____ my friend Jack. He is from Hong Kong in

② _____. He is not like me. I am from ③ _____, and I

am studying ④ _____. Jack loves ⑤ _____.

He is taking classes in ⑥ _____ and literature. Jack is always

happy and ⑦ _____. He's living at home and taking classes

⑧ _____ this semester, so we aren't hanging out as much as usual

these days.

---

literature = novels, poems, plays, etc.
hang out = to spend time with a friend

Practice reading the text clearly. Talk to a partner, or record the answer.

Vocabulary Review

Review the vocabulary from Unit 3. Write new words in your vocabulary notebook. You can listen to them on the book's companion website.

accent	evidence	monster
American	France / French	nervous
angry	gas	online
attractive	Germany / German	personality
battery	Great Britain / British	Poland / Polish
Canada / Canadian	hang out	pollution
canceled	happy	relieved
century	impatient	sad
China / Chinese	India / Indian	Scotland / Scottish
confident	Ireland / Irish	South Africa / South African
confused	Italy / Italian	the United States (the U.S.)
country	Korea / Korean	the United Kingdom
due on	legend	(the U.K.)
electric	literature	tired
England / English	lively	turn in
enthusiastic	lunar	Wales / Welsh
Europe / European	Mexico / Mexican	worried

Spelling Skills

Change the order of the letters to form words from Unit 3. The first one has been done for you as an example.

1. papyh   _happy_

2. rietd   _____

3. sveruon _____

4. llyive   _____

5. rowdier _____

UNIT 4

Describing Places

Learning Targets	Importance on the iBT
Vocabulary —Education —Around town *Vocabulary Skill:* Using a dictionary	• **iBT:** understand and use words about education, which are frequent on the iBT • **iBT Reading and Listening:** understand geography passages
Grammar —Prepositions —*If/when* sentences (present/future)	• **iBT:** understand and use prepositions correctly • **iBT Speaking and Writing:** use conditional sentences to describe places and give advice
Speaking Clearly —Consonant sounds / l / and / r /	• **iBT Speaking:** pronounce difficult sounds correctly for better delivery • **iBT Listening:** recognize words by identifying the correct sound

Getting Started

Discuss these questions.

1. Close your eyes. Describe the room you are in now. What is in the room? Who else is there? What do you do there?

2. What is your favorite place in your home town? Why?

Vocabulary You Need

I. Education

Study this map of a typical U.S. university campus.

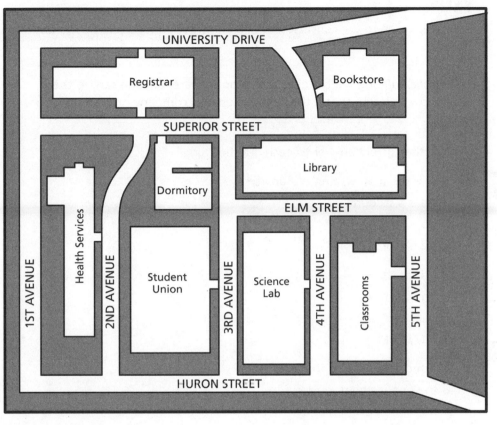

Exercise 4.1

Where on campus should these people go? Choose places from the map. The first one has been done for you as an example.

1. I feel sick.   Health Services
2. I'm meeting friends for coffee.   _____
3. I'm going to my room.   _____
4. I have an English class.   _____
5. I have a problem with my schedule.   _____
6. I need to get a book for my paper.   _____
7. I'm buying my textbooks.   _____
8. I have a chemistry experiment today. _____

Step Up Note: *Some conversations on the listening and speaking sections of the iBT take place on North American university campuses.*

EXERCISE 4.2

Track 18. Listen to the conversation at a university visitor's center. You can take notes.

> *public building* = a building that is not private, anyone can go there
> *logo* = a design that is the official sign of a company or organization

Choose the correct answer to each question.

1. Why is the man visiting the university?
   a. He is a student.
   b. He is the parent of a student.
   c. He is a professor.

2. Which of these can you do at the student union, according to the woman?
   a. drink coffee
   b. sleep
   c. buy books

3. Which cafeteria does the man go to?
   a. the one in the dormitory
   b. the one near the library
   c. the one near the classroom building

4. What does the man do after he leaves the visitor's center?
   a. turns left
   b. turns right
   c. goes straight ahead

5. Where can the man buy a university t-shirt?
   a. the bookstore
   b. the library
   c. the visitor's center

Exercise 4.3

Complete the vocabulary webs using words from the box. Each web contains words
from a school subject.

geography	dates	poems	experiments	business

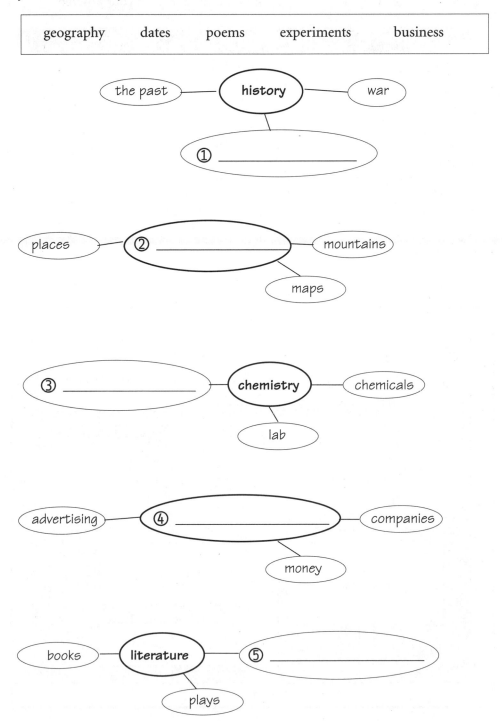

the past — **history** — war

① _____

places — ② _____ — mountains

maps

③ _____ — **chemistry** — chemicals

lab

advertising — ④ _____ — companies

money

books — **literature** — ⑤ _____

plays

EXERCISE 4.4

Look at the chart. Check (✓) **Like** or **Dislike** for each school subject. Then, give a reason for each opinion. Discuss with a friend, or record your answers.

Subject	Like	Dislike	Reason
1. history			
2. science			
3. foreign languages			
4. art			
5. math			

II. Around Town

Look at the town map.

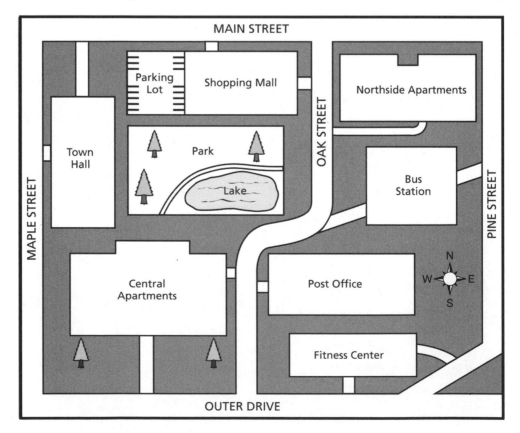

Step Up Note: *One style of Reading to Learn question on the reading section of the iBT asks you to fill in a chart, such as the one in Exercise 4.5.*

EXERCISE 4.5

Track 19. Look at the map on page 48. Listen to the conversation in a university housing office. You can take notes.

> *traffic* = cars, buses, trucks, etc.
> *convenient* = practical; easy
> *lease* = a contract to rent an apartment

1. Complete the chart with information about the two apartments. You will not use two of the answer choices.

Northside Apartments	1. _____
	2. _____
Central Apartments	3. _____
	4. _____

   a. close to the shopping mall

   b. near a train station

   c. a lot of traffic

   d. near a lake

   e. convenient for public transportation

   f. convenient to the university

Choose the correct answer for the questions.

2. Which apartments does the woman choose?

   a. Northside Apartments

   b. Central Apartments

   c. Southside Apartments

3. Why does the woman want to live near the park?

   a. She likes swimming.

   b. She likes walking.

   c. She likes jogging.

4. What is the rent for the apartment she chooses?

   a. $400 a month

   b. $700 a month

   c. $800 a month

5. When can she move in to the apartment?

   a. The lease starts on June 1.

   b. The lease starts on July 1.

   c. The lease starts on July 4.

EXERCISE 4.6

1. Draw a simple map of your hometown.

2. Describe your hometown. What do you like about it? Give reasons for your opinion. Talk for about a minute; record your answer if possible.

Vocabulary Skill: Using a Dictionary

To improve your English and prepare for the iBT, you need a good learner's dictionary. When you look up a new word, find out as much as you can about it. For example, for the word *convenient*, you can learn:

- the part of speech (*adjective*)
- if it is frequently used (*yes*)
- the pronunciation—underline the stressed syllable (/ kən-<u>vin</u>-yənt /)
- the meaning, in clear simple English (*practical, easy, comfortable*)
- example sentences (*The apartments are convenient for public transportation.*)
- how to use the word (something is *convenient*; a person can't be *convenient*)
- similar or opposite words (*inconvenient*)
- other members of the word family (*conveniently, convenience*)

Grammar You Can Use

I. Prepositions

> "Today, though, **for** those of us who live **in** a country where there is a fast food restaurant **on** every corner, this process actually is beginning to harm us."
>
> —*The Michigan Guide to English for Academic Success and Better TOEFL® Test Scores*, p. 262

Prepositions are small words that sometimes describe where a thing is. Look at the campus map on page 45.

The Dormitory is **next to** the Student Union.

The Health Services is **opposite** the Student Union.

The classroom building is **near** the Library.

When you leave the Dormitory, the Registrar is **in front of** you.

The Bookstore is **behind** the Library.

 Exercise 4.7

Complete the sentences using the correct preposition from the box.

outside	behind	beside	above	from

1. The desk is in front of the window. The window is _____ the desk.

2. The bed is under the light. The light is _____ the bed.

3. The TV is next to the plant. The plant is _____ the TV.

4. The people are inside the house. The car is _____ the house.

5. The sofa is opposite the door. The door is across _____ the sofa.

iBT

EXERCISE 4.8

Read the description of the human ear, and look at the diagram. *Don't* look up the words in *italics* in your dictionary.

Inside your ear, you find the *ear canal*. Sound travels through the ear canal to the *eardrum*. The *hammer* is above the eardrum, and the *anvil* is behind the hammer. When sound reaches the eardrum, the hammer and the anvil vibrate. The *cochlea* is below the hammer and anvil. When the hammer and anvil vibrate, the cochlea sends a signal to the brain.

vibrate = to move up and down very quickly

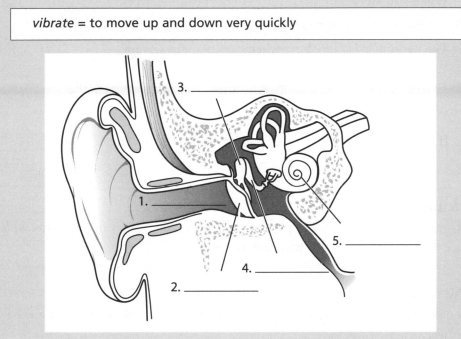

Write the parts of the ear on the correct line in the diagram.

a. eardrum
b. anvil
c. cochlea
d. ear canal
e. hammer

Step Up Note: Many reading and listening passages on the iBT contain technical words that you do not need to know because they are explained in the passage. However, it is important to understand them using context. (You will not complete a diagram on the iBT.)

II. *If/When* Sentences

"**When** a language dies, so do cultural stories, history, and heritage. **When** we lose language, we lose a piece of history."

—*The Michigan Guide to English for Academic Success and Better TOEFL® Test Scores*, p. 135

You use *if/when* **sentences** in the present and future tenses to describe a situation that happens or will happen *if* or *when* something else happens.

If you go out of the library, you will see the bookstore.

When you are feeling sick, you go to the health services.

I walk past the cafeteria **when** I go to class.

The parking lot is very busy **when** classes are in session.

You can also use *if/when* sentences to give advice:

If you want a good lunch, try the restaurant on Main Street.

Watch Your Step!

- Don't use *will* in the *if/when* part of the sentence: do not say or write, *You will see the bookstore when you **will** go out of the library.*

The Next Step

- Look at the commas in the example sentences. Use a comma only when the *if/when* clause comes at the beginning.

Exercise 4.9

Combine the two sentences into an if/when *sentence. The first one has been done for you as an example.*

1. You're looking for an apartment. Try Central Apartments.

   <u>If you're looking for an apartment, try Central Apartments.</u>

2. You reach the student union. Turn left.

   _____

3. I eat in my room. The cafeteria is closed.

   _____

4. You like to study in a quiet place. I recommend the library.

   _____

5. You live in a small town. You meet a lot of people.

   _____

EXERCISE 4.10

Track 20. Listen to the professor talking at the end of a class. You can take notes.

> *final paper* = a long essay at the end of a university course
> *elevator* = a machine that takes you up and down in a building
> *slide* = to move smoothly on a surface

Choose the correct answer to each question.

1. When are the papers due?
   a. Wednesday
   b. Thursday
   c. Friday

2. What is one way the Professor does NOT want to receive the papers?
   a. in Wednesday's class
   b. by email
   c. at his office

3. Where is the professor's office?
   a. on the third floor of Brock Hall
   b. when you go into Brock Hall
   c. when you get out of the elevator

4. When do you turn left?
   a. when you go into Brock Hall
   b. when you come out of the elevator
   c. when you get to Office 312

5. Where can students leave their papers if the office is locked?
   a. behind the door
   b. beside the door
   c. under the door

Speaking Clearly

Consonant Sounds: / l / and / r /

The sounds / l / as in *left* and / r / as in *right* are difficult for some learners to pronounce. When you say / l /, touch your tongue to the top of mouth. When you say / r /, don't touch anything in your mouth with your tongue.

Exercise 4.11

Practice reading the sentences.

1. Turn left at the classroom building.

2. The registrar is right.

3. I like drinking lemonade.

4. The rent is really low.

5. The library is near the lake.

Track 21. Listen, and repeat the sentences.

iBT

EXERCISE 4.12

Prepare to answer this question: **Do you prefer living in a large town or a small town?** Give reasons for your answer.

1. Do you prefer living in a large town or a small town? _____

2. Write three reasons for your answer. You can use the words in the box.

convenient	parks	apartments	lots of people	more/less traffic

a. 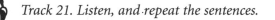_____

_____

b. _____

_____

c. _____

_____

3. Circle all the / l / and / r / sounds in your answers to Questions 1 and 2.

4. Answer the question: Do you prefer living in a large town or a small town? Give reasons for your answer. Pay attention to your / l / and / r / sounds. Talk for about 45 seconds; record your answer if possible.

Vocabulary Review

Review the vocabulary from Unit 4. Write new words in your vocabulary notebook. You can listen to them on the book's companion website.

above	experiment	park
access	final paper	parking lot
across from	fitness center	play
advertising	geography	poem
apartment	health services	post office
art	history	public building
behind	in front	public transportation
beside	inside	registrar
bookstore	lake	rent
bus station	languages	schedule
business	lease	science lab
cafeteria	library	shopping mall
campus	logo	slide
cashier	map	textbook
chemical	money	traffic
chemistry	mountains	tuition
company	near	under
convenient	next to	vibrate
dormitory	opposite	visitor's center
downtown	outside	war
elevator		

Spelling Skills

Write the correct letters in the words from Unit 4.

1. s ____ ____ ____ nce lab

2. visitor's ce ____ ____ ____ r

3. shopping m ____ ____ ____

4. post off ____ ____ ____

5. public tran ____ ____ ____ rtation

UNIT 5

Describing Your Experiences

Learning Targets	Importance on the iBT
Vocabulary —Strong verbs —School words *Vocabulary Skill:* Understanding roots	• **iBT Independent Writing:** Use strong verbs to tell an interesting story as supporting evidence • **iBT Speaking:** use a wide range of vocabulary • **iBT:** understand and use school or university vocabulary, which is frequent on the iBT
Grammar —The simple past tense —Irregular verbs	• **iBT Reading and Listening:** understand passages set in the simple past tense • **iBT Independent Writing:** write about your experience using the simple past tense and irregular verbs
Speaking Clearly Pronouncing the *-ed* ending	• **iBT Speaking:** use the simple past tense ending when you are telling a story • **iBT Listening:** understand the time sequence of a lecture or conversation by recognizing past and present tenses

Getting Started

Discuss these questions.

1. Describe a memory from your childhood. Where were you? Who was there? What happened? Why is it important to you now?

2. What do you do every day at school?

Vocabulary You Need

I. Strong Verbs

You will score better on the iBT writing and speaking sections if you use strong verbs to describe actions or feelings. Strong verbs, such as *notice* or *argue*, describe a specific action or feeling. Weak verbs, such as *be, do, have,* and *get,* do not include any new information. Avoid overusing weak verbs. Notice the difference in the two sentences.

When I **am** in school, I **have** conversations with my friends.	OK
When I **go** to class, **eat** lunch, and **play** sports, I **chat** with my friends.	Better

Exercise 5.1

Write each strong verb in the appropriate column. The first two have been done for you as examples.

~~chat~~	~~walk~~	notice	run	arrive
observe	leave	interrupt	argue	discuss

Verbs like *move*	Verbs like *talk*	Verbs like *see*
walk	chat	

iBT

EXERCISE 5.2

Read the paragraph. It could be the answer to an independent speaking task on the iBT.

When you have a homework assignment,
do you start early or wait until the last minute?

In my experience, it is better to wait until the last minute. I ⓐ <u>am</u> at my desk, and I ⓑ <u>have</u> my things—paper, pens, notes, computer. My notes already ⓒ <u>have</u> the information. I ⓓ <u>do</u> the assignment quickly. Then, I ⓔ <u>have</u> a short break. If mistakes ⓕ <u>are</u> in my answer, I ⓖ <u>do</u> a second draft.

> *until the last minute* = right before the deadline
> *draft* = a piece of writing that is not finished

1. Replace each underlined word in the paragraph with a strong verb from the box. Use each word once. Use a dictionary to help you.

contain	write	prepare	sit	appear	complete	take

   a. _____

   b. _____

   c. _____

   d. _____

   e. _____

   f. _____

   g. _____

2. When you have a homework assignment, do you start early or wait until the last minute? Describe how you complete an assignment. Use strong verbs. Talk for about 30 seconds; record your answer if possible.

II. School Words

Read Kristin's **schedule** for Monday.

9:00	Chemistry **lab**
10:00	Geography lecture (**quiz** today on **unit** 2 from the textbook)
12:00	English class (**assignment** due today)
1:00–3:00	**Review** for Tuesday's math test
4:00	History **seminar** (Nora's **presentation**)

Exercise 5.3

Complete the sentences using the words in bold from Kristin's schedule.

1. A _____ is a list of everything you do during the day.

2. A small test is called a _____.

3. A _____ is a class with a small number of advanced students.

4. To study for a test, you _____ your notes.

5. You do experiments in a _____ (or laboratory) class.

6. When you give a _____, you stand in front of the class and talk about a topic.

7. A section in a textbook is called a _____.

Step Up Note: Question 3 on the iBT integrated speaking task asks you to read a short passage and then listen to a lecture or conversation on the same topic.

iBT

EXERCISE 5.4
Read this notice from a university:

What Is Your Major?
All **sophomore** students must **declare** their **major** by May 1. If you do not know your major yet, please talk to your **advisor.** You cannot **register** for classes without a major.

1. Match the vocabulary words in the announcement with the correct meaning.

   1. _____ sophomore   a. choose
   2. _____ declare   b. person who helps students
   3. _____ major   c. second-year student
   4. _____ advisor   d. sign up for a class
   5. _____ register   e. main subject you study

Track 22. Listen to the conversation between a student and his advisor. You can take notes.

> *graduate* = to finish university (or high school)
> *grades* = final scores in your classes

2. Are these statements true or false? Place a check (✓) in the correct column.

	True	False
a. The student likes computer science more than business.		
b. The student has good grades in computer science and business.		
c. The student wants to work for a technology company when he graduates.		
d. The student can choose two majors.		
e. The university offers a minor in computer science.		
f. The university offers a minor in business.		

3. Explain what the student chooses for a major and minor, and why. Talk for about 30 seconds; record your answer if possible.

Vocabulary Skill: Understanding Roots

Many academic English words come from Latin or Greek. These words often have a *root*—a base word. If you learn some common roots, you can guess the meaning of other related words.

Root	Meaning	Examples
-spec-	look	*spectator* (person who watches) *spectacles* (glasses) *spectacular* (amazing to look at)
-logo-	science / study	*sociology* (study of society) *biology* (study of life)
-divers-/-divert-	different	*diversity* (a variety of different people or things) *divert* (send someone a different way)
-rupt-	break, tear	*interrupt* (break into a conversation) *eruption* (when a volcano explodes)

Grammar You Can Use

I. The Simple Past Tense

The **simple past** tense describes an action or event that finished in the past. Use the simple past tense when you describe an experience or story from the past.

"In Athens, in Greece, for example, democracy **differed** from Roman government. In Athens, every citizen **voted** for every decision—in contrast to Rome, where an emperor **made** many decisions."

—*Step Up to the TOEFL® iBT for Intermediate Students*, p. 171

Simple Present	Simple Past
I play tennis.	I **played** tennis.
You look happy.	You **looked** happy.
He studies history.	He **studied** history.
They live in Canada.	They **lived** in Canada.

The negative form of the simple past tense uses *did not* (in formal writing) or *didn't* (in speaking or informal writing): *I **did not like** the food. He **didn't know** that.*

The Next Step

- In verbs that are more than one syllable long and end in *r*, we double the *r* in the simple past tense (for example, *I prefer* ➔ ***I preferred***).
- In verbs that end in **y,** the **y** changes to **i** (for example, *I study* ➔ I ***studied***).

EXERCISE 5.5

Complete the paragraph with the simple past form of the correct verb from the box. This could be one paragraph in an independent writing task on the iBT. The first one has been done for you as an example.

~~study~~	learn	watch	listen	help	type

When I was in high school, I ① _studied_ Spanish. I ② _____

a lot of grammar in class, and we ③ _____ Spanish and Mexican

movies. I also ④ _____ to Spanish radio stations. My uncle

speaks very good Spanish, so he ⑤ _____ me a lot. I was very

proud when I ⑥ _____ my first essay in Spanish!

Exercise 5.6

Answer the questions in complete sentences using the simple past tense.

1. Did you play a musical instrument when you were younger?

   _____

2. When did you start English classes?

   _____

3. What movie did you watch recently?

   _____

4. How did you travel to school today?

   _____

5. Did you enjoy the weekend?

   _____

iBT

EXERCISE 5.7

Read the passage about travel agents.

In the past, most people booked vacations, airplane tickets, and hotel rooms through a travel agent. The travel agent reserved the tickets and collected the money. The agent also received some money because he or she advised travelers on good hotels and trips. Now, most people buy their tickets online, and there are not many travel agents. So, you have to work harder to plan a trip, but you will usually save money.

> *book* = to reserve a hotel room, tickets for a flight, etc.
> *collect* = to take
> *receive* = to get

Choose the correct answer to each question.

1. According to the reading, which of these did people NOT book through a travel agent?
   a. hotel rooms
   b. theater tickets
   c. travel tickets

2. When you reserved tickets with a travel agent, who did you give your money to?
   a. the travel agent
   b. a website
   c. The passage doesn't say.

3. Do most people use travel agents today?
   a. yes
   b. no
   c. The passage doesn't say.

4. What is a disadvantage of booking tickets online?
   a. You pay less money.
   b. You don't book good hotels.
   c. You do more work.

5. Complete the chart with information from the reading. Write the statements in the correct box. You will not use two of the answer choices.

Travel agents	1. _____
	2. _____
	3. _____
Travel websites	1. _____
	2. _____

a. Most people used them in the past.

b. Most people use them today.

c. They only booked hotel rooms.

d. They advised travelers.

e. Travelers save money.

f. They are not safe.

g. They bought the tickets.

Step Up Note: The question in Exercise 5.8 is similar to one you could see as the independent writing task on the iBT.

iBT

EXERCISE 5.8

Prepare to write about this question: **Who was your favorite teacher, and why?**

1. Write the name of your favorite teacher: _____

2. What subject did he or she teach?
   _____

3. When were you in this class? _____

4. What did you learn from this teacher? Write three details.

   a. _____

   b. _____

   c. _____

5. On a separate sheet of paper, write a few sentences to describe an experience in class when you learned *one* of the things in Question 4.

6. Use the answers to Questions 1–5. In your notebook, write your answer to this question: **Who was your favorite teacher, and why?**

II. Irregular Verbs

Some common English verbs are **irregular**. This means that they do not form the simple past tense by adding -ed. You need to learn these verbs. For a longer list of irregular verbs, please see Appendix B.

Present	Past	Present	Past
I am	I was / you were*	I think	I thought
I have	I had	I tell	I told
I go	I went	I know	I knew
I do	I did	I see	I saw
I say	I said	I teach	I taught
I get	I got	I feel	I felt
I come	I came	I give	I gave
I make	I made	I write	I wrote

* The verb *be* is the only verb with two forms in the simple past tense: *I/he/she/it was*, but *you/we/they were*. All other verbs have one form for all subjects in the simple past.

The Next Step

- Some irregular verbs have irregular pronunciation. For example, the simple past tense of *read* (pronounced / rid / like the verb *need*) is *read* (pronounced / rɛd / like the color *red*).

Exercise 5.9

Complete the sentences with the simple past form of the correct irregular verb. The first one has been done for you as an example.

~~be~~   give   feel   teach   write   get   do

1. My first-grade teacher _____was_____ Mr. Lomas.

2. He _____ me math and English.

3. He _____ a lot of homework.

4. I _____ many essays.

5. I also _____ a lot of math problems.

6. At the end of the class, I _____ a good grade.

7. I _____ good because I understood both English and math!

EXERCISE 5.10

Read the paragraph, which could be part of an answer to an independent writing question on the iBT. The question is: **Should school children wear uniforms?** There are some mistakes in the verbs.

When I were in elementary school, we have a uniform. We weared gray shorts, a white shirt, and black shoes. I hated it! We all find ways to break the rules. For example, one of my friends always had brown shoes, not black. The teachers was always angry with us. However, another one of my friends go to a school with no uniform. The students chose their own clothes. They do not break the rules, and they were much happier than us. Therefore, uniforms are bad for discipline.

---

uniform = a set of clothes that everyone must wear
elementary school = school for children from ages 5 to 10
break the rules = to do something wrong
discipline = good behavior

---

1. Underline all the verbs in the paragraph.

2. Look at each verb. Should it be in the simple present or simple past tense? Is it regular or irregular?

3. Correct all the mistakes. There are seven mistakes. Use the list of irregular verbs in Appendix B to help you.

Speaking Clearly

Pronouncing the *-ed* Ending

There are three ways to pronounce the *-ed* ending on regular simple past tense verbs:

/ d /	/ t /	/ ɪd /
played	*looked*	*wanted*

You can predict the correct pronunciation:
- If the last sound of the base form of the verb is *voiced* (*b, d, g, z, m, n, v, y, l, r, w, ž, ǰ, ð,* or any vowel), pronounced / d / (*played, studied, seemed*).
- If the last sound is *unvoiced* (*t, p, k, s, f, š, č, θ, h*), pronounced / t / (*looked, watched, typed*).
- If the last sound is / t / or / d /, pronounced /ɪd/ (*wanted, needed, started*).

For a complete list of voiced and unvoiced sounds, see Appendix A, Phonetic Symbols.

Exercise 5.11

Track 23. Listen to the simple past tense verbs in the sentences. Place a check (✔) in the correct box for the ending that you hear.

	/ d /	/ t /	/ ɪd /
1. I <u>washed</u> the car this morning.			
2. He <u>lived</u> in Europe as a child.			
3. I <u>traveled</u> to school by bus.			
4. I <u>completed</u> my assignment last night.			
5. You <u>learned</u> to play the guitar in high school, didn't you?			

Practice saying the sentences. Check your pronunciation with the audio CD.

Step Up Note: On the iBT, you have 15 seconds to prepare for questions like these. You can only write a few words—don't try to write your speech!

iBT

EXERCISE 5.12

Answer the questions using the simple past tense. Make short notes before you start speaking. Talk for about 45 seconds; record your answers if possible. Pronounce the -*ed* endings carefully.

1. What was your favorite vacation? Where did you go? What did you do?

   Notes: _____

   _____

2. What is your strongest childhood memory? Where were you? Who was there? What happened?

   Notes: _____

   _____

3. What was the last movie you saw? What happened in it? Did you like it?

   Notes: _____

   _____

Vocabulary Review

Review the vocabulary from Unit 5. Write new words in your vocabulary notebook. You can listen to them on the book's companion website.

advisor	eruption	reserve
appear	grades	review
argue	graduate	run
arrive	interrupt	save money
assignment	irregular	seminar
biology	lab/laboratory	sophomore
book	leave	spectacles
break the rules	major	spectacular
chat	minor	spectator
collect	musical instrument	study
computer science	notice	test
contain	observe	the last minute
declare	prepare	travel agent
discipline	presentation	type
diversity	quiz	uniform
divert	receive	unit
draft	register	walk
elementary school		

Spelling Skills

Correct the spelling mistakes in the words from Unit 5.

1. boilogy   _____

2. buisness   _____

3. papear   _____

4. recieve   _____

5. tipe   _____

UNIT **6**

Giving Reasons

Learning Targets	Importance on the iBT
Vocabulary —Likes and dislikes —Service encounters *Vocabulary Skill:* Understanding prefixes and suffixes	• **iBT Reading and Listening:** understand likes and dislikes and reasons for them • **iBT Writing and Speaking:** give reasons for your opinions • **iBT Listening; Integrated Writing and Speaking:** understand service encounter conversations
Grammar —Asking questions —Conjunctions	• **iBT Listening:** listen for questions that require reasons as answers, especially in service encounters and conversations • **iBT Writing and Speaking:** connect ideas using conjunctions for improved organization
Speaking Clearly —Consonant sounds / š /, / č /, / ž /, / ǰ /	• **iBT Speaking:** pronounce these sounds correctly for better delivery • **iBT Listening:** recognize words by identifying the correct sound

Getting Started

Discuss these questions.

1. What school subjects do you like? Why?

2. What do you like to do in your free time? Why?

Vocabulary You Need

I. Likes and Dislikes

You often need to say what you like or don't like and give a reason. Here are some words you can use.

Verbs		Adjectives	
like	don't like	fun	boring
prefer	dislike	exciting	dull
love	hate	pretty	ugly
enjoy	don't care for	awesome	awful

Some adjectives describe only some nouns. For example, a building can be *high* or *tall*, but a person is *tall*, not *high*.

Exercise 6.1

Complete each sentence with a word from the box. Use a different word for each sentence. Make the sentences true for you.

1. I _____ cooking.

2. I _____ playing sports.

3. My friend _____ writing.

4. For me, reading books is _____.

5. Today, my friend is wearing _____ shoes.

iBT

EXERCISE 6.2

Track 24. Listen to the conversation between a student and her professor. The student is writing a *term paper*—a long essay due at the end of the semester. You can take notes.

> *cell* = the smallest part of a living thing
> *nutrition* = the study of food and eating
> *energy* = the power to do something with your body

Choose the correct answer to each question.

1. What subject is the professor probably teaching?
   a. English literature
   b. biology
   c. education

2. Why does the student talk to her professor?
   a. She does not understand the class.
   b. She does not eat vegetables.
   c. She does not have a topic.

3. Track 25. Listen again to part of the conversation. What did the student enjoy in the class?
   a. cells
   b. the human body
   c. nutrition

Step Up Note: You will sometimes listen again to part of a lecture or conversation on the listening section of the iBT.

4. Why did she enjoy the topic?
   a. She loves eating vegetables.
   b. She learned to eat better.
   c. The professor is a good teacher.

5. What is the student's question for her paper?
   a. How can we teach young people about good nutrition?
   b. What is good nutrition?
   c. Do you enjoy eating vegetables?

Exercise 6.3

Write sentences to answer the questions. Give a reason for each answer. The first one has been done for you as an example, but write your own answer to this question.

1. What sports do you like?

   I enjoy soccer because it's a team sport, and I really love to play with

   other people.

   Your answer: _____

   _____.

2. Do you prefer living in a city or in the country?

   _____.

   _____.

3. What is your favorite food?

   _____.

   _____.

4. What is your favorite subject at school?

   _____.

   _____.

5. What is your ideal (=*perfect*) job?

   _____.

   _____.

II. Service Encounters

The listening, speaking, and writing sections of the iBT may include conversations between students and university employees. These are called **service encounters**. If you live in North America, you will have many of these service encounters yourself. You read about academic advising in Unit 5. Here are some words you might use in other situations on campus.

Housing Office	Cashier's Office	Secretary's Desk	Library
dorm	tuition	fill out	check out
period (of time)	fees	form	return
sign up	credit card	error / mistake	renew
roommate	check	mail (a letter)	fine
assignment	cash	apply	recall
single / double	bill	confirm	library card

Some of these words are useful in several situations, of course!

Exercise 6.4

Track 26. Listen to the conversations, and complete the table. The first one has been done for you as an example.

supervisor = manager, boss

	Where does it take place?	What does the student want?	Can the other person help? (yes or no)
1	housing office	change his roommate	No
2			
3			
4			
5			

Exercise 6.5

Match the questions on the left with the appropriate answers on the right.

1. _____ How can I pay my bill?

2. _____ Can I renew this book?

3. _____ Would you like a single or double room?

4. _____ Where do I sign up for classes?

5. _____ Why do I pay student fees?

a. Sorry. Someone else asked for it.

b. For the fitness center, computer labs, and health services.

c. By cash or check.

d. You can register online.

e. I'd prefer to have a roommate.

EXERCISE 6.6

Track 27. Listen to the conversation at a university housing office. You can take notes. Choose the correct answer to the questions.

1. What is the woman's problem?
   a. She doesn't like her dorm room.
   b. Her dorm room is too expensive.
   c. She hates her roommate.

2. What kind of room does she have for next year?
   a. a single room
   b. a double room
   c. an off-campus apartment

3. Which of the following does the housing officer NOT suggest?
   a. live with a roommate
   b. live off campus
   c. find a cheaper dorm building

4. What is the advantage of an off-campus apartment?
   a. a private room
   b. more rent
   c. a nice room

5. Track 28. Listen again to part of the conversation. Is the woman going to choose an off-campus apartment?
   a. yes
   b. no
   c. maybe

iBT

EXERCISE 6.7

What is your advice for the woman in Exercise 6.6? Make notes.

1. Which is the best option for her? _____

2. Write two reasons:

    a. _____

    b. _____

3. Do you have a personal experience with a situation like this? What happened?

    _____

    _____

Step Up Note: Question 4 is similar to Task 5 on the integrated speaking part of the iBT.

4. What should the woman in Exercise 6.6 do? Explain your opinion, and give reasons for your answer. Talk for about 30 seconds; record your answer if possible.

Vocabulary Skill: Understanding Prefixes and Suffixes

In Unit 5, you read about roots. English words can also include *prefixes* (at the beginning of words) and *suffixes* (at the end of words). Most prefixes add meaning to the word. Most suffixes change the part of speech of a word. Here are some common prefixes and suffixes.

Prefix	Example	Suffix	Example
re- (again)	replay, repeat	*-tion/-sion* (noun)	information, question
co-/col- (together)	cooperate, collaborate	*-ize* (verb)	recognize, realize
dis- (not, completely different)	disaster, disappear	*-al* (adjective)	electrical, practical
anti- (against)	anti-guns, antisocial	*-ly* (adverb)	quickly, rarely

Grammar You Can Use

I. Asking Questions

You will hear a lot of questions in the listening section of the iBT and also in the integrated tasks. You will probably not ask questions during the test, but it is still an important skill in real life. There are three main types of questions.

> "When students come to a university, most live on campus in a dormitory, while some choose to live farther from campus in an apartment. **Would** you prefer to live in a dormitory or apartment. **Why**?"
>
> —adapted from *The Michigan Guide to English for Academic Success and Better TOEFL® Test Scores*, p. 235

1. **Yes/No Questions:**

    With main verbs: *Do you like the book?*

    With helping verbs: *Are you a student here?*

2. ***Wh-* Questions (*who, where, what, why, when, how*):**

    With main verbs: *Why do you like math?*

    With helping verbs: *Where are you going?*

3. **Tag questions:**

    With main verbs: *You agree, don't you?*

    With helping verbs: *This is the library, isn't it?*

Watch Your Step!

- Use *does* with *he/she/it* in the simple present tense. Use *did* with all subjects in the past simple tense.
- Use the base (bare infinitive) form of the verb in yes/no and *wh-* questions: *Does he like English?* not **Does he like̶s̶ English?*)

The Next Step

- You can use a **tag question** to check that you are right. For example, if you think you're in front of the library, you might ask another student: *This is the library, isn't it?* Your voice goes **up** a little at the end.
- Other times, you're certain that you are right. For example, if you're complaining about a new rule at the university, you say to your friend: *That's terrible, isn't it?* Your voice goes **down** a little at the end.

Exercise 6.8

Track 29. Listen to the questions. You will hear each question twice. Choose the most logical and grammatical answer.

1. a. It's near the post office.

   b. Yes, it is.

   c. It's a library.

2. a. an hour ago

   b. by bus

   c. I have a chemistry class.

3. a. Yesterday

   b. No, I was sick.

   c. It was great!

4. a. Yes. How can I help you?

   b. Yes. Turn left and walk two blocks.

   c. No thank you.

5. a. I prefer tennis.

   b. very much.

   c. It helps me relax.

Exercise 6.9

Write a question for each answer. The first one has been done for you as an example.

1. <u>Who is your history professor?</u>

   I have Dr. Park for history this semester.

2. _____

   It's next to the library and opposite the bank.

3. _____

   I like classical music because it's relaxing.

4. _____

   Yes, I eat here every day.

5. _____

   That's right. I have a really nice roommate.

Step Up Note: Students sometimes ask questions during lectures and classes on the listening section of the IBT. Some questions ask the professor to explain an idea or give a reason. Other questions present a different opinion. Pay attention to the professor's answers!

EXERCISE 6.10

Track 30. Listen to part of an economics class. You can take notes. Use your notes to choose the correct answer to each question.

> *purchases* = things you buy
> *charge* = to ask a particular amount of money for something
> *annual* = every year
> *80 percent* = 8 out of 10

1. What is the main question that the professor is answering?

   a. Why do people use credit cards?

   b. How do credit card companies make money?

   c. Why do stores take credit cards?

2. What is interest?

   a. a credit card fee

   b. a type of credit card

   c. money you pay when you borrow money

3. How do credit card companies make money if you pay your bill in full?

   a. They charge you interest.

   b. They charge you fees.

   c. They don't make money.

4. Which of these fees does the professor NOT mention?

   a. a fee to pay your bill online

   b. a late fee

   c. a fee to use the card every year

5. When do store owners pay money to the credit card companies?

   a. when they use a credit card

   b. when they buy something online

   c. when a customer uses a credit card

6. Why do most stores take credit cards?

   a. Many people use credit cards.

   b. Credit cards are expensive.

   c. They don't want to pay fees.

II. Conjunctions

Conjunctions connect ideas. Some conjunctions show reasons and causes. Others show contrasts, new ideas, or effects. If you understand conjunctions, you can follow the meaning of the writer or speaker. Here are some common conjunctions.

> "The problem is complicated by the make-up of fat **and** muscle tissues. Fat **and** muscle are two different types of tissue. Fat, **or** adipose tissue, is made up of lipids."
>
> —*The Michigan Guide to English for Academic Success and Better TOEFL® Test Scores*, p. 261

Conjunction	Meaning	Example
and	addition	*Good computers are fast **and** expensive.*
but	contrast	*Cell phones are useful, **but** they don't always work.*
so	result	*Email is convenient, **so** many people use it.*
or	choice	*Do you prefer Italian **or** French food?*
because	reason	*The Internet is important **because** it connects information.*

 The Next Step

- *And, or, but,* and *so* are called **coordinating conjunctions**. They can connect nouns, verbs, adjectives, or whole sentences. When they connect sentences, use a comma before the conjunction.
- *Because* is a **subordinating conjunction**. It can only connect sentences. If *because* is in the middle of a sentence, do not use a comma.

iBT

EXERCISE 6.11

Read the passage about a famous opera. An opera is a play with classical music and singing. Circle all the conjunctions in the passage.

Madame Butterfly is one of the most popular operas today, but it was not popular at its first performance in 1904. At that time, people cheered during an opera because they liked it, but no one cheered for *Madame Butterfly*. In fact, the audience hated the opera, so they shouted bad things at the singers and the writer. Because the first audience did not enjoy *Madame Butterfly*, it closed after that performance. Later, audiences loved the opera, and now there are many performances of the opera every year.

cheer = to shout happily
audience = people who watch a play or opera
performance = show

Choose the correct answer to each question.

1. Which of these sentences is the main idea of the passage?
   a. *Madame Butterfly* was popular from its first performance.
   b. The audience did not like the first performance of *Madame Butterfly*.
   c. *Madame Butterfly* was not popular at first, but it is very popular now.

Step Up Note: Although there is no main idea question on the reading section of the iBT, understanding the main idea will help you answer the negative fact and summary questions.

2. Why did people cheer during an opera in the 1900s?
   a. They liked the opera.
   b. They hated the opera.
   c. They had no opinion about the opera.

3. What happened at the first performance of *Madame Butterfly*?

   a. The audience shouted good things.

   b. The singers shouted at the audience.

   c. The audience shouted bad things.

4. Why did the opera close after the first performance?

   a. The audience hated it.

   b. The opera was bad.

   c. The audience loved it.

5. Which of these statements is true?

   a. There are no performances of *Madame Butterfly* today.

   b. There was only one performance of *Madame Butterfly*.

   c. *Madame Butterfly* is a very popular opera today.

Exercise 6.12

Complete the sentences with the correct conjunction. Use each conjunction only once.

because	and	or	so	but

1. I like singing because it's fun, _____ I'm good at it.

2. When I'm older, I want to be an actor _____ a business owner.

3. I played football as a child, _____ I prefer baseball these days.

4. I enjoy hiking, _____ I want to live in the country.

5. Homework is important _____ it helps me remember my lessons.

Speaking Clearly

Consonant Sounds: / š /, / č /, / ž /, / ǰ /

These four sounds are quite similar, but you need to pronounce them correctly, or people will not understand you.

/ š /   is the sound in <u>sh</u>ip, <u>sh</u>ow, wa<u>sh</u>, nutri<u>ti</u>on

/ č /   is the sound in <u>ch</u>ip, wa<u>tch</u>, tea<u>ch</u>er

/ ž /   is the sound in plea<u>su</u>re, ga<u>ra</u>ge, vi<u>si</u>on

/ ǰ /   is the sound in <u>j</u>ump, ve<u>g</u>etables, a<u>ge</u>

Here are some tips to help you pronounce the sounds:

- / š / and / č / are unvoiced, but / ž / and / ǰ / are voiced (see Unit 5).
- Your tongue does not touch the top of your mouth when you say / š / and / ž /.
- Make a / t / sound at the start of the / č /.
- Make a / d / sound at the start of the / ǰ /.

Watch Your Step!

- The / ž / sound is unusual because it is never the first sound in an English word.

Exercise 6.13

Track 31. Listen to the words. Place a check (✓) in the correct column for the sound that you hear.

	/ š /	/ č /	/ ž /	/ ǰ /
1. children				
2. television				
3. shout				
4. passage				
5. lunch				
6. section				
7. measure				
8. check				
9. adjective				
10. information				

 Listen again, and repeat the words.

EXERCISE 6.14

Track 32. Listen to the paragraph. It could be the answer to an independent speaking question on the iBT.

Do you enjoy watching television?
Why or why not?

I don't watch television any more. I just watch my favorite shows online. I enjoy watching videos on the Internet because I choose the time to watch them. I usually tune in late at night to catch up. And I watch shows from different places: Asia, Germany, or Brazil. I get more information, and I see almost no commercials.

> *tune in* = to turn on a TV show
> *catch up* = to watch something you missed
> *commercials* = ads on TV

1. Underline all the / š /, / č /, / ž /, and / ǰ / sounds in the paragraph.

2. Practice reading the underlined words. Check your pronunciation with the audio CD.

Vocabulary Review

Review the vocabulary from Unit 6. Write new words in your vocabulary notebook. You can listen to them on the book's companion website.

annual	credit card	percent
apply	don't care for	performance
audience	dull	period (of time)
awesome	energy	pretty
bill	error / mistake	purchases
boring	fees	recall
cash	fill out	renew
catch up	fine	return
cells	form	roommate
charge	ideal	secretary
check	library card	sign up
check out	mail	single / double room
cheer	measure	supervisor
classical music	mistake	term paper
commercials	nutrition	tune in
confirm	opera	ugly

Spelling Skills

Change the order of the letters to form words from Unit 6.

1. ahsc _____

2. citxenig _____

3. geerny _____

4. trerun _____

5. papyl _____

UNIT 7

Giving Opinions

Learning Targets	Importance on the iBT
Vocabulary —Opinion words —Adverbs *Vocabulary Skill:* Guessing from context	• **iBT:** understand opinions in reading and listening passages on all sections of the test • **iBT Speaking and Writing:** give your opinion using correct vocabulary
Grammar —Comparatives —Modal verbs	• **iBT:** understand and express opinions using comparisons • **iBT:** recognize and use modal verbs to express opinions
Speaking Clearly —Word stress	• **iBT Speaking:** stress the correct syllable for better comprehension • **iBT Listening:** recognize words using syllable stress

Getting Started

Discuss these questions.

1. Do you think libraries are important today?

2. In your opinion, is text messaging (texting) good or bad for teenagers?

Vocabulary You Need

I. Opinion Words

You will hear and read a lot of opinions in academic lectures and readings. You also need to give your opinion in speaking and writing. Here are some opinion words and phrases.

> I **think that** libraries are important.
>
> I **believe that** libraries are important for university students.
>
> **In my opinion**, we can get more information from the Internet.
>
> **According to** my teacher, the Internet has a lot of bad information.
>
> Libraries are **important / necessary / essential**.
>
> Books are **unimportant / old-fashioned / boring**.
>
> Librarians are **great / awesome / cool / amazing**.
>
> That's a **terrible / awful / crazy / ridiculous** idea!

iBT

EXERCISE 7.1

Read the paragraph, which could be part of an answer to an independent writing task on the iBT. *Weblogs* (or *blogs*) are personal websites. Anyone can write his or her ideas and opinions in a blog for other people to read and comment on.

What is your opinion of blogs?

In my opinion, blogs are a great idea, especially for college students. I believe that college students have to learn to think for themselves. Blogs are important because you can write your opinion in them. Other people can give feedback, and this is essential because you discover if other people agree with you. Blogs are better than diaries, in my opinion. Diaries are old-fashioned. They are private, but young people want to express themselves in public. Overall, I think blogs are really cool!

> *feedback* = other people's comments, good or bad
> *discover* = to learn, find out
> *diary* = a book in which you write about your life

1. Underline all the words that show the writer's opinion.

2. Answer the questions about the paragraph.

   a. Does the writer think blogs are good or bad? _____

   b. Who should have a blog, according to the writer? _____

   c. What are his two reasons?

      i. _____

      ii. _____

   d. What are blogs better than? _____

   e. Why? _____

   f. What word does the writer use to begin his conclusion? _____

3. Write a paragraph to answer the question with your opinion. Use the questions in Number 2 as a guide.

What is your opinion of cell phones?

_____

_____

_____

_____

_____

_____

_____

_____

_____

Exercise 7.2

Track 33. Listen to different students answer the question: Do you think the legal driving age should be increased to 18 years old? *(In the U.S., most teenagers can learn to drive at the age of 16.)*

1. What is each student's opinion? Place a check (✓) in the correct column.

Student	Good Idea	Bad Idea
1.		
2.		
3.		
4.		

2. Replay Track 33. Listen again to each student's answer. Write the correct opinion words next to the student who said them.

good	I think	better
No way!	Yes, I do!	I don't think so.
terrible	I don't know.	in my opinion

Student 1: _____   _____

_____

Student 2: _____   _____

Student 3: _____   _____

Student 4: _____   _____

II. Adverbs

Adverbs are words that describe verbs, adjectives, other adverbs, or describe whole sentences. Sometimes, adverbs show an opinion.

> Teenagers should <u>drive</u> **carefully.**
>
> That is **completely** <u>ridiculous</u>!
>
> You're talking **too** <u>quickly</u>.
>
> **Unfortunately,** I <u>can't help you.</u>

 ### Exercise 7.3

Read the sentences. The underlined words are adverbs. Match the adverb to the correct meaning. The first one has been done for you as an example.

1. __i__ There are no buses on Sunday. <u>Fortunately</u>, I like walking!

2. ____ <u>Unfortunately</u>, I can't help you.

3. ____ Some people think that all fats are bad for you. But <u>actually</u>, some fats are good for your health.

4. ____ That's <u>absolutely</u> right!

5. ____ I think 8 AM is <u>too</u> early to start classes.

6. ____ There <u>aren't enough</u> people here to play soccer. We need eleven players.

7. ____ "My next class is math." "<u>Really</u>? I thought you were in my math class."

8. ____ <u>Maybe</u> I'd like living in a big city, but I've always lived in the country.

9. ____ You <u>probably</u> can't learn vocabulary by reading a dictionary.

a. in fact (the first idea is wrong)
b. too few
c. possibly; I'm not sure
d. completely; certainly
e. I'm not happy about this.
f. I'm surprised; I didn't know that.
g. over the limit
h. I'm almost certain (but not completely).
i. I'm pleased about this.

Step Up Note: *Some questions on the listening section of the iBT ask you to identify the speaker's emotion—for example, surprised, happy, etc.*

EXERCISE 7.4

Track 34. Listen to the conversation between a student and a teaching assistant. You can take notes. Use your notes to choose the correct answer to each question.

> *extra credit assignment* = additional work done to improve your grade
> *flexible* = able to change
> *strict* = tough; not flexible

1. What does the student want to talk about?

   a. a quiz

   b. the professor

   c. a paper

2. Why didn't the student get a good grade?

   a. He was absent.

   b. He was tired from playing sports.

   c. He did not understand the class.

3. Track 35. Listen again to part of the conversation. Which of the statements about the teaching assistant is correct?

   a. She does not want to give the student an extra-credit assignment.

   b. She is happy that she cannot make a decision about the assignment.

   c. She wants to help, but she has to ask the professor.

4. Will the professor agree to the student's request, according to the teaching assistant?

   a. absolutely not

   b. maybe

   c. probably

5. Why is the student surprised?

   a. He thinks the professor is not flexible.

   b. He knows the professor is flexible.

   c. He thinks the teaching assistant is strict.

6. What is the student going to do next?

   a. talk to the professor

   b. write to the teaching assistant

   c. write to the professor

Exercise 7.5

Choose the correct sentence to complete each short conversation.

1. Do you want to see a movie tonight?

   a. Absolutely! What's showing?

   b. I really like movies.

2. Let's study for the quiz together.

   a. Really? What are you doing?

   b. Actually, I have a class now. Can we study later?

3. Did you buy the textbook?

   a. No, it's too expensive.

   b. Yes, it's too expensive.

4. I didn't study hard enough for today's quiz.

   a. Unfortunately, today's class is canceled.

   b. Fortunately, today's class is canceled.

5. I'm playing on the university soccer team this weekend.

   a. Actually, I love watching soccer.

   b. Really? I didn't know you played soccer!

Vocabulary Skill: Guessing from Context

Sometimes, when you don't know a word, you can guess its meaning by looking at other words. This is called guessing from context. This is a very important skill, especially on the iBT reading section. You will not know all the words in the passages, but you can guess the general meaning of some new words. Here are some ways to guess from context.

1. Look for a similar word in the sentence.

   She looks happy and **contented**.

   Guess: *contented* is similar to *happy*.

2. Look for the opposite word nearby, after a word like *but* or *however* or *not*.

   The food sounded **unappetizing**, *but it tasted great.*

   Guess: *unappetizing* means it doesn't taste good.

3. Use the logic (for example, time, sequence, place) of the sentence to help you guess.

   Tokyo is a busy **metropolis**.

   Guess: I already know that Tokyo is a big city, so *metropolis* probably means the same.

   We look after our students from **matriculation** *to graduation.*

   Guess: Graduation is at the end of a university degree, so *matriculation* is the start of your studies at a university.

Grammar You Can Use

I. Comparatives

> "In a twin and family study, researchers are looking to see if people who are **more** related tend to resemble each other **more than** people who are **less** related."
>
> —*The Michigan Guide to English for Academic Success and Better TOEFL® Test Scores*, p. 261

Comparatives are words used to show a degree of comparision.

There are two ways to make a comparison with an adjective.

1. *My university is* **bigger than** *my home town.*

   Add *-er* to short adjectives (1 or 2 syllables).

2. *Studying is* **more important than** *playing sports.*

   Use *more . . . than* with long adjectives (2 or more syllables).

You can also make comparisons with other parts of speech.

I like skiing **more than** running.

There are **more** facilities at a large university **than** a small school.

I need to work **harder.**

Newspapers bring the news **more slowly than** the Internet.

 *Watch Your Step!*

- There are **two important irregular comparative adjectives:**

  good → better   bad → worse

- Double the consonant and add *-er* when the word ends with one vowel + consonant (*big* → *bigger*).

Exercise 7.6

Complete the sentences with the comparative form of the word in parentheses.

1. (small)   I would prefer to buy a _____ car.

2. (interesting) I think videos are _____ than photographs.

3. (useful)   Blogs are _____ than email.

4. (slowly)   I read _____ than some of my friends.

5. (books)   I have to read _____ this year than last year.

EXERCISE 7.7

Read the passage about the English language. Then choose the correct answer to each question.

How many words?

There are more than 600,000 words in the English dictionary, and more words are added every year. However, one organization believes the English language is growing faster than that. They say there are more than one million words and phrases in English. Some experts disagree and think this is a ridiculous number because it includes two-word phrases. In fact, there are more phrases than anyone can count—certainly more than one million. So, the smaller number of words in the dictionary is probably more accurate.

organization = group of people doing a particular job
expert = a person who knows a lot about a subject

1. How many words are in the English dictionary, according to the reading?

    a. about 400,000

    b. 500,000

    c. more than 600,000

2. What happens to the number of words in the dictionary every year?

    a. It becomes smaller.

    b. It becomes bigger.

    c. It does not change.

3. Who says that the English language is growing faster?

    a. the dictionary

    b. a language organization

    c. no one

4. How can the organization say the language is larger than the dictionary?

    a. by including names

    b. by including foreign words

    c. by including words and phrases

5. Why do experts disagree with the organization?

    a. It is impossible to count all the two-word phrases in English.

    b. It is impossible to count all the words in English.

    c. The dictionary is always right.

6. What does the word *accurate* in the last sentence mean?

    a. interesting

    b. unusual

    c. correct

Step Up Note: You will always answer a question like Number 6 on the reading section of the iBT. The target word is highlighted in the passage.

Exercise 7.8

Think about a friend or family member. How is this person different from you? Talk for about a minute; record your answer if possible.

II. Modal Verbs

Modal verbs add extra information to a sentence. They often show the speaker's or writer's opinion. Modal verbs have many meanings.

"You **can** register online, but you **must** have the permission of the classroom instructor. You **may not** take the same course twice for credit. If you have questions, you **should** call your departmental advisor."

—possible reading passage on iBT integrated speaking question

Meaning	Modal	Example
Possibility	**can** (more certain) **could** (less certain)	Television **could affect** children's language development.
Necessity	**must, have to** (strong) **should** (weak)	We **must find** new sources of energy.
Ability	**can** (present) **could** (past)	When I was younger, I **could play** the piano.

Watch Your Step!

- Modal verbs do not change: He *can* swim is possible, but He *cans* swim is not.
- *Have to* is a different kind of verb, but it has a similar meaning to *must*. Remember to say: *We have **to go*** and *We must **go**, but not *We must to go.*

The Next Step

- Other modal verbs include *will, would, may,* and *might*.
- Other verbs like *have to* include *be able to, be supposed to,* and *need to*.

Exercise 7.9

Rewrite the sentences with a modal verb. The first one has been done for you as an example.

1. Working in a group is better than working by yourself.

   <u>Working in a group can be better than working by yourself.</u>

2. Members of a group work together.

   _____

3. People make mistakes.

   _____

4. A group of people considers many ideas.

   _____

5. A group makes better decisions than individuals.

   _____

EXERCISE 7.10

Track 36. Listen to the conversation between two students about choosing a dormitory room. You can take notes. Use your notes to choose the correct answers to each question.

> *room assignment* = room selection

1. What is the main topic of the conversation?
   a. the cost of housing
   b. finding a roommate
   c. choosing a dormitory building

2. What does the woman have to do this week?
   a. choose a room assignment
   b. register for classes
   c. talk to her roommate

3. Which dorm building can the woman NOT choose?
   a. River Building
   b. Smith Building
   c. Jones Street

4. Which building is older than the others?
   a. River Building
   b. Smith Building
   c. Jones Street

5. Which building does the woman choose?
   a. River Building
   b. Smith Building
   c. Jones Street

6. Where does the woman have to go to complete her room assignment form?
   a. her dormitory room
   b. the cashier's office
   c. the housing office

 Exercise 7.11

Write answers to the questions. Use modal verbs. The first one has been done for you, but write your own answer to this question.

1. Do you like playing sports? Why, or why not?

   <u>I like some sports like golf because you can get exercise, and you</u>

   <u>have to learn the technique.</u>

   Your answer: _____

   _____

2. How old should teenagers be when they learn to drive?

   _____

   _____

3. Do you think all college students should study a foreign language? Why, or why not?

   _____

   _____

Speaking Clearly

Word Stress

When a word has more than one syllable, one syllable has the **word stress**. Stressing the right syllable is sometimes more important than pronouncing the sounds correctly. You can use a dictionary to check the stress of many words. However, here are some general patterns.

Most long nouns	Stress first syllable	_address, radio, textbook_
Most long verbs	Stress second syllable	_consider, record_
Most words with suffixes	Stress the syllable before the suffix	_information, assignment, assistant_
Most words with prefixes	Don't stress the prefix	_reply, dislike_

The stressed syllable is a little louder, higher, and slower than other syllables. (For more information about prefixes and suffixes, see page 82.)

Exercise 7.12

Track 37. Listen, and underline the stressed syllable in the words.

1. opinion
2. ridiculous
3. important
4. dormitory
5. decision

6. university
7. building
8. conversation
9. expensive
10. absolutely

iBT

EXERCISE 7.13

Track 38. Listen to the conversation between two students. They are discussing a problem with a group project for an economics class. You can take notes.

> *economics* = the study of money, trade, and industry
> *cooperate* = to work together
> *solve* = to fix a problem

1. Write short answers to these questions.

   a. What is the problem in the group?

   _____

   b. What are the two solutions that the woman suggests?

   i. _____

   ii. _____

2. Listen again to the conversation. (Repeat Track 38.) Underline the stressed syllable in the key words.

   a. economics   e. together

   b. project   f. groupmate

   c. problem   g. connect

   d. cooperate   h. solution

Step Up Note: *Part 3 of the exercise is similar to an integrated speaking task on the iBT.*

3. What should the man do about this problem? Choose one of the solutions, and explain why you think this is the better solution. Try to use correct word stress in your answer. Talk for about 45 seconds; record your answer if possible.

Vocabulary Review

Review the vocabulary from Unit 7. Write new words in your vocabulary notebook. You can listen to them on the book's companion website.

absolutely	expert	organization
accurate	extra-credit	private
actually	assignment	probably
amazing	feedback	project
awful	flexible	really
believe	fortunately	ridiculous
blog	great	room assignment
connect	important	stress
context	in my opinion	strict
cool	legal driving age	terrible
cooperate	maybe	think
crazy	necessary	too
diary	no way	unfortunately
discover	not enough	unimportant
economics	old-fashioned	

Spelling Skills

Write the correct letters in the words from Unit 7.

1. In my opi ____ ____ ____ n, fall is nicer than spring.

2. Unfor ____ ____ ____ ately, we cannot play outside today.

3. I am working on an interesting geography pro ____ ____ ____ t.

4. You're a ____ ____ ____ lutely correct.

5. We need to c ____ ____ ____ erate on our group presentation.

Summarizing

Learning Targets	Importance on the iBT
Vocabulary —Sequence words —Contrast words *Vocabulary Skill:* Recognizing collocations	• **iBT Integrated Speaking:** summarize an opinion and reasons; summarize and connect a reading and listening; summarize a situation • **iBT Integrated Writing:** summarize a lecture and relate to the reading, sometimes by contrasting the two • **iBT Reading:** use sequence and contrast words to answer "insert text" questions
Grammar —Superlatives —Articles	• **iBT all sections:** recognize and use superlatives to organize information in a passage or summary • **iBT Writing and Speaking:** use articles accurately
Speaking Clearly —Sentence stress	• **iBT Speaking:** use correct sentence stress for improved delivery • **iBT Listening:** find main ideas by recognizing sentence stress

Getting Started

Discuss these questions.

1. Talk or write about a book you read recently. What was the book about?

2. What did you learn from reading this book? Write your answer in one to three sentences.

Vocabulary You Need

I. Sequence Words

The summary tasks on the iBT ask you to present information in a clear order. You can do this with sequence words. Here is a list of common sequence words.

First, . . .	**Second**, . . .	**Third**, . . .
The **first** point is	The **next** problem is . . .	The **last** solution is . . .
One problem is..	**Another** solution is . . .	**Finally**, . . .
The professor says . . .	**In addition**, . . .	**Furthermore**, . . .

Sometimes, you can begin your answer with a preview sentence. A preview sentence tells the listener what to listen for. Here are some possible preview sentences.

The student has **two problems**.
The professor makes **two suggestions**.
The woman has **three reasons**.
There are **three differences** between the reading and the lecture.

The Next Step

- Some sequence words are more common in writing than in speaking. We don't usually use words like *furthermore* or *in addition* in speaking, but they are good words in writing.
- Sequence words are very useful for summaries, but when you give your opinion about a topic, try not to use *first, second, third*. Explain **why** the ideas are in this sequence.

Exercise 8.1

Read the passage. Add different sequence words from the boxes to complete the sentences.

There are three problems with Internet telephones. The ① _____

problem is quality. Your voice sounds clearer on a regular telephone.

② _____, you cannot use the telephone if you lose your Internet

connection. ③ _____, if you call 911, the emergency services

might not be able to see your address quickly.

911 = the telephone number for fire, police, or ambulances in the U.S.
emergency services = fire, police, and ambulance (for serious health problems)

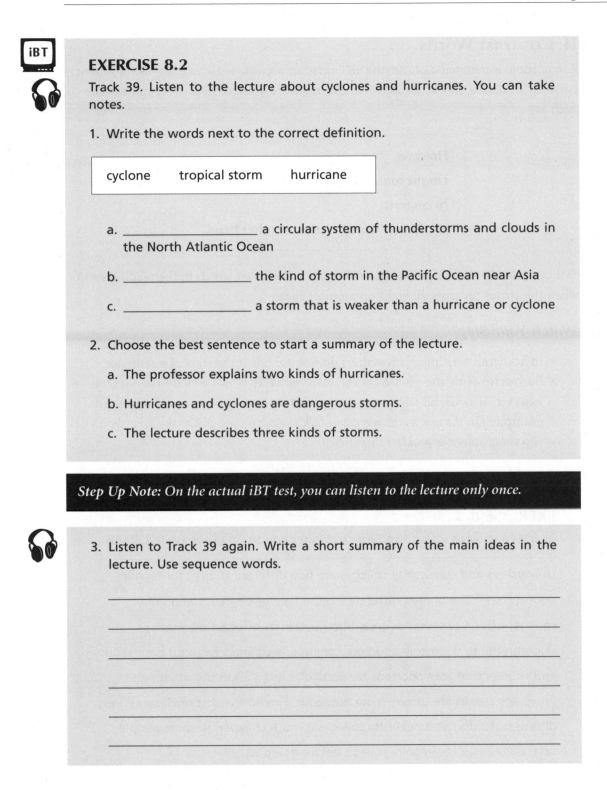

EXERCISE 8.2

Track 39. Listen to the lecture about cyclones and hurricanes. You can take notes.

1. Write the words next to the correct definition.

cyclone   tropical storm   hurricane

a. _____ a circular system of thunderstorms and clouds in the North Atlantic Ocean

b. _____ the kind of storm in the Pacific Ocean near Asia

c. _____ a storm that is weaker than a hurricane or cyclone

2. Choose the best sentence to start a summary of the lecture.

a. The professor explains two kinds of hurricanes.

b. Hurricanes and cyclones are dangerous storms.

c. The lecture describes three kinds of storms.

Step Up Note: On the actual iBT test, you can listen to the lecture only once.

3. Listen to Track 39 again. Write a short summary of the main ideas in the lecture. Use sequence words.

_____

_____

_____

_____

_____

_____

II. Contrast Words

A common integrated task on the iBT writing section is to explain the differences between a lecture and a reading. You can organize your writing with *contrast words*, such as:

> **However,**
>
> **On the contrary,**
>
> **In contrast,**
>
> **On the one hand, . . . On the other hand,**

You can also use the conjunction *but*. You will see contrast words in the reading section when the writer presents different opinions or ideas.

 Watch Your Step!

- In academic writing, many writers do not use *but* at the start of a sentence.
- Be careful with the phrase *on the other hand*. It is not exactly the same as *however*. It is useful when you are presenting two options or solutions. For example: *On the one hand, you could talk to your professor. On the other hand, you could solve the problem by yourself.*

iBT

EXERCISE 8.3

Read the passage about two types of higher education in the United States.

Universities and community colleges are two different choices for higher education. ⒈ The biggest difference is the type of degree: community colleges offer a two-year degree, but universities offer a four-year undergraduate degree. In addition, community colleges focus on basic skills and courses that are important for particular jobs. ⒉ On the other hand, university classes are usually more academic. Finally, the cost of classes is very different. Tuition at community colleges is much cheaper, so some people take classes at a community college before going to university. ⒊

Choose the correct answer to each question.

1. What is the main idea of the reading?

   a. Universities are better than community colleges.

   b. Universities and community colleges are the same.

   c. There are differences between universities and community colleges.

2. According to the reading, where can you get a degree?

   a. at a university only

   b. at a community college only

   c. at both a university and a community college

3. Which of these statements is true, according to the reading?

   a. Community colleges are more expensive than universities.

   b. University degrees take longer than community college degrees.

   c. University classes are more difficult than community college classes.

4. Why do some people study at a community college before going to university?

   a. They can save money.

   b. They can save time.

   c. They can get a better degree.

Step Up Note: *You will see questions like Question 5 on the reading section of the iBT.*

5. Look at the three squares (□). What is the best place to add this sentence?
   However, other students prefer to take all their classes at a university.

   a. ①

   b. ②

   c. ③

EXERCISE 8.4

Track 40. Read the passage in Exercise 8.3 again. Listen to part of the lecture. The professor is talking about a new choice in high school called an Early College. You can take notes. Use your notes to choose the correct answer to the questions.

traditionally = usually; in the past
earn money = to make money from a job

1. Check (✓) all the ideas that are in the lecture.

   a. _____ Access to higher education is a big problem today.

   b. _____ Everyone can pay for community college classes.

   c. _____ Some people don't go to college because it is too expensive.

   d. _____ Other students don't go into higher education because they want to get a job.

   e. _____ In an early college, you take community college classes in high school.

   f. _____ You can get a four-year degree in high school.

   g. _____ You can get a community college degree in high school.

   h. _____ You can continue studying at university after an Early College high school.

2. Summarize the ideas in the lecture. You can make notes below, but don't write full sentences. Talk for about 30 seconds; record your answer if possible.

   _____

   _____

   _____

Step Up Note: Question 2 is similar to the last integrated speaking question on the iBT.

3. How is the Early College High School in the lecture different from the types of higher education in the reading in Exercise 8.3? Complete the sentences in this paragraph.

The reading presents two choices for higher education after high school. However, the lecture describes ⓐ_____ _____. Both colleges and universities cost money. However, ⓑ_____ _____. Finally, the degrees in the reading take two to four years after high school. On the other hand, ⓒ_____ _____.

Step Up Note: Question 3 is similar to one kind of integrated writing task on the iBT.

Vocabulary Skill: Recognizing Collocations

Collocations are words that go together. It is important to learn words in phrases because your writing and speaking will be more accurate. Here are some types of collocation.

Verb + preposition: **study at** a university; **go to** high school
Adjective + preposition: I'm **interested in** biology.
Noun + preposition: There's a **problem with** my class.
Verb + noun: **earn money**
Adjective + noun: **severe weather**

Look and listen for collocations, and write them in your vocabulary notebook.

Grammar You Can Use

I. Superlatives

"Cyrus the Great united the two original Iranian tribes, the Medes and the Iranians. So, he founded this empire which was one of **the largest** empires on earth."

—*The Michigan Guide to English for Academic Success and Better TOEFL® Test Scores*, p. 272

In Unit 7, you learned about comparatives, such as *bigger* and *more important*. Comparatives are used to compare two things.

A **superlative** describes the *number one* out of many things. Here are some examples:

China has **the largest** population in the world.

The biggest problem for most students is the cost of tuition.

Your advisor is **the most important** person for you at the university.

Other superlatives describe sequence.

The **first** part of the lecture is about dogs.

Superlatives are possible with other parts of speech, but they are less common.

The team with **the most points** wins.

Who can finish the exercise **most quickly**?

▰▰▰ *Watch Your Step!*

- When you use a superlative adjective with a noun, always start with *the*.
- Two irregular superlatives are: *the best* (most good) and *the worst* (most bad).

Exercise 8.5

Complete the sentences with the superlative form of one of the adjectives in the box. Use each adjective once.

important	good	useful	happy	low

1. You should buy the computer with _____ price.

2. _____ advice is to take good notes during lectures.

3. My writing class was _____ course I took during my first year of college. It helped me in all my other classes.

4. I think _____ solution is to find a new roommate.

5. The day I met my baby brother was _____ day of my life!

EXERCISE 8.6

Read a student's summary of a lecture on business. There are four mistakes in the use of superlatives. Find the mistakes, and correct them.

According to the lecture, there are three difficulties for service companies. The most first problem is communication. Companies have to find new ways to get information to their customers. The second problem is loyalty. This is the most big difficulty. The goodest companies keep their customers for a long time, but this is harder for service companies. Finally, service companies cannot prepare for an increase in demand. This is the more important difficulty for companies in very competitive industries because they could lose customers.

loyalty = the quality of staying with someone or something
competitive = trying to be more successful than other people or companies

EXERCISE 8.7

Answer the questions. Use superlatives in your answers. Talk for about 45 seconds for each question; record your answers if possible.

1. What is most important for you when choosing a job?

2. What is the best way to listen to music: on the radio, on MP3 players, or at concerts?

3. In some classes, you write many essays. In other classes, you write one big essay. And in others, you take an exam at the end. What is the best way for teachers to test and grade students?

II. Articles

"Evidence from various sources points to **a** significant climactic role for solar disturbances, particularly for **the** absence of any."

—*The Michigan Guide to English for Academic Success and Better TOEFL® Test Scores*, p. 9

Articles (*a, an, the*) are possibly the most difficult part of English grammar. However, you can reduce your mistakes by following some guidelines.

1. Singular, countable nouns must have an article. Countable nouns can be plural and mean specific *things*, not categories: *a table, a question, the test.*

2. Generally, *a/an* means *any* one thing. Only singular countable nouns can take *a/an: a problem, a choice, an opinion.*

3. Generally, *the* means *this* one or group exactly. Any common noun can take *the: the questions on the test; the people in the room; the library; the water in the oceans.*

4. We often use *no article* (Ø) with non-count nouns (*grammar*), proper nouns (*Chicago*), school subjects (*history*), and plural nouns (*difficulties*) when the meaning is general.

Your understanding of articles will improve as you study more English, so try to notice articles as you read.

Watch your Step!

• Choosing between *a* and *an*: Use *a* in front of most words; use *an* only in front of a word starting with a vowel sound: *an apple, an hour, an orange pen.*

 ## Exercise 8.8

Complete the sentences with the correct words from the box.

problems   an apple   the lecture   a good idea   the cafeteria

1. I'm going to _____. Are you hungry?

2. _____ is about early English drama.

3. There are _____ with this idea.

4. Finally, you should eat _____ every day.

5. I agree with the woman: group work is _____.

Exercise 8.9

Choose the correct article from the choices in parentheses. The symbol Ø means no article.

1. (The / a) first point is about the cost of education.

2. I saw (a / the) great movie last week. (A / The) movie was a Japanese horror film.

3. Today's lecture is about (the / Ø) environment.

4. The speaker is a professor of (the / Ø) economics.

5. (The / Ø) people in the study were students at (a / the) large university.

EXERCISE 8.10

Track 41. Listen to the conversation between a student and a professor. You can take notes. Use your notes to choose the correct answer to each question.

> *section* = one class group in a large course
> *open* = (of a class) not full

1. What is the conversation about?
   a. a problem with the professor's class
   b. a problem with the student's schedule
   c. a problem with a physics class

2. What subject does the professor teach?
   a. art
   b. physics
   c. math

3. How many art classes are open next semester?
   a. none
   b. one
   c. two

4. Track 42. Listen again to part of the conversation. How many sections of the physics class are open next semester?
   a. one
   b. two
   c. many

5. Which physics class does the student decide to take?
   a. 8 AM
   b. 10 AM
   c. 11 AM

Exercise 8.11

Track 43. Listen again to part of the conversation from Exercise 8.10. Complete the conversation with the correct article: a, an, *or* the.

> *Professor:*   Mine is ① _____ only art class next semester. Can you change your physics class? Are there other sections of ② _____ class?
>
> *Student:*   Yes, there are ③ _____ lot of sections, but only two are still open. There's ④ _____ 8 AM section. That's so early!
>
> *Professor:*   Well, I think you have ⑤ _____ choice. If you want to take my art class, you must take ⑥ _____ 8 AM physics class.

Speaking Clearly

Sentence Stress

In Unit 7, you saw that words have a major stress. Sentences also have a main stress—one of the stressed syllables has a little bit **more** stress than the others. Usually, the **sentence stress** is on the last content word (noun, verb, adjective, or adverb).

> *The first problem is <u>time</u>.*
> *The student wants a new <u>room</u>mate.*

However, sometimes the sentence stress is on the newest or most important information. For example:

> *There are <u>three</u> main points in the lecture.*
> *I <u>don't</u> agree with the student.*
> *I think he should take the <u>mor</u>ning class.*

When two contrasting ideas are in a sentence, both words can have equal stress

> *The woman is studying <u>his</u>tory, but the man is studying <u>phy</u>sics.*

> **Step Up Note:** *The paragraph in Exercise 8.12 could be the answer to Question 5 on the speaking section of the iBT. You will hear a conversation about a problem. Then, you summarize the situation and give your opinion about the best solution.*

EXERCISE 8.12

Read the paragraph.

The conversation is about the woman's roommate. She wants a different roommate. The man suggests talking to the housing office. However, she wants to talk directly to her roommate. The best solution is talking to her roommate. I think she should be honest. She wants to be friends with her roommate. So, they have to agree. I think the roommate might want to move. Then, they'll both be happier.

> *honest* = telling the truth

1. Underline one word or syllable in each sentence that you think has the sentence stress.

2. Track 44. Listen to the paragraph. Check your answers. There are different possible answers.

3. Practice reading the passage aloud.

EXERCISE 8.13

Track 45. Listen to part of a lecture about food allergies. An allergy is a bad reaction to eating certain foods. You can take notes.

> *risk* = danger

1. Make notes in the table about the two opinions:

	Most Doctors	Other Doctors
What does the child eat?	No nuts before 2 years old.	
Good result		
Problem		

Step Up Note: *Question 2 in this exercise is similar to Question 6 on the speaking section of the iBT.*

2. Explain the difference between the two opinions about treating children with nut allergies. Use sentence stress and contrast words to make your answer clear. Talk for about one minute; record your answer if possible.

Vocabulary Review

Review the vocabulary from Unit 8. Write new words in your vocabulary notebook. You can listen to them on the book's companion website.

class section	honest	on the one/other hand
community college	however	open
competitive	hurricane	risk
cyclone	in addition	second
degree	in contrast	severe
earn money	last	third
emergency services	loyalty	thunderstorm
finally	next	traditionally
first	on the contrary	tropical storm
furthermore		

Spelling Skills

Correct the spelling mistakes in the underlined words from Unit 8.

1. Music is a <u>competive</u> industry.   _____

2. It is hard to <u>ern</u> money as an artist.   _____

3. <u>Howevr</u>, there are many examples of successful musicians.   _____

4. <u>Frist,</u> you need a good business plan.   _____

5. You can <u>finaly</u> succeed.   _____

Appendix A: Phonetic Symbols

Track 46

Note: A short vowel sound comes after each consonant so you can hear the consonant better.

Consonants		
Unvoiced	*Voiced*	*Nasal (voiced)*
p put, appear, sheep	b bill, maybe, robe	m meal, amazing, seem
t tin, eaten, right	d do, older, head	n no, answer, ran
k cat, account, stick	g get, ago, egg	ŋ anger, sing,
f feel, effect, laugh	v very, over, wave	swimming
θ thin, three, math	ð this, either, with	
s sit, listen, serious	z zip, easy, days	
š ship, wishes, fish	ž pleasure, vision, garage	
č chin, matches, rich	ǰ just, suggest, age	
h have, hair, behind	w was, awesome, few	
	l left, allow, real	
	r right, arrow, four	
	y you, player	
Vowels		
i feet, me, see		u boot, choose, cool
ɪ bit, lip, hid		ʊ book, look, took
e wait, say, name	ə the, sofa, pizza	o boat, note, soak
ɛ wet, set, let	ʌ but, cup, about	ɔ all, tall, author
æ cat, ad, hand		a not, on, hot
ay right, fine, type	ɔy boy, toy, annoy	aw now, round, out

Appendix B: Common Irregular Verbs

Base Form	Past Simple Tense
be	was / were
become	became
begin	began
break	broke
bring	brought
build	built
buy	bought
catch	caught
choose	chose
come	came
cost	cost
cut	cut
do	did
draw	drew
drink	drank
drive	drove
eat	ate
fall	fell
feel	felt
fight	fought
find	found
forget	forgot
freeze	froze
get	got
give	gave
go	went
grow	grew
have	had
hear	heard
hide	hid
hold	held
hurt	hurt
keep	kept
know	knew
lead	led
leave	left

Base Form	Past Simple Tense
let	let
lose	lost
make	made
mean	meant
meet	met
pay	paid
put	put
quit	quit
read	read
ride	rode
ring	rang
rise	rose
run	ran
say	said
see	saw
sell	sold
send	sent
set	set
shoot	shot
shut	shut
sing	sang
sit	sat
sleep	slept
speak	spoke
spend	spent
stand	stood
steal	stole
swim	swam
take	took
teach	taught
tell	told
think	thought
understand	understood
wake	woke
wear	wore
win	won
write	wrote

Vocabulary Index

All 392 vocabulary items are in the top 2,000 most frequent words in English (the General Service List; see To the Teacher, p. xii), except proper nouns and words marked:

* = word is on the Academic Word List
† = word is not on the Academic Word List or the General Service List

Answer Key

Unit 1: Stepping Up to the iBT

Exercise 1.1 (page 2)

2. directions   3. passages   4. integrated   5. opinion

Exercise 1.2 (page 3)

1. b   2. a   3. c   4. b   5. a

Exercise 1.3 (page 4)

1. b   2. a   3. b   4. c   5. a

Exercise 1.4 (page 5)

2. mainly   3. describe, mention, discuss   4. specific   5. according to
6. hold   7. author   8. topics

Exercise 1.5 (page 6)

2. a   3. e   4. b   5. d   6. f

Exercise 1.6 (page 7)

Check items 2, 4, 6

Exercise 1.7 (page 8)

Answers will vary. Sample responses:

2. Choose   3. Summarize   4. Explain   5. Include   6. Ask

Exercise 1.8 (page 8)

Answers will vary.

Exercise 1.9 (page 10)

2. main verb   3. adjective   4. helping verb   5. adverb

Exercise 1.10 (page 10)

2. main   3. summary   4. writer   5. completely

Exercise 1.11 (page 11)

2. 1   3. 2   4. 4   5. 2   6. 3   7. 2   8. 1

Exercise 1.12 (page 12)

1. study   2. mainly   3. write   4. explain   5. describing

Spelling Skills (page 13)

1. sections   2. complete   3. example   4. essential   5. conversation

Unit 2: Talking about Yourself

Exercise 2.1 (page 15)

2. grandfather   3. brother-in-law   4. cousins   5. great grandfather

Exercise 2.2 (page 16)

2. c   3. a   4. b   5. a   6. b

Exercise 2.3 (page 17)

Answers will vary.

Exercise 2.4 (page 18)

Answers will vary.

Exercise 2.5 (page 19)

1. c   2. b   3. c   4. c   5. b

Exercise 2.6 (page 20)

Answers will vary.

Exercise 2.7 (page 21)

2. play   3. teaches   4. get   5. watch

Exercise 2.8 (page 22)

1. b   2. c   3. a   4. b

Exercise 2.9 (page 23)

1. is   2. stop   3. are   4. need

Exercise 2.10 (page 23)

Some people prefer <u>having</u> a large family. For example, my friend has five siblings. She loves <u>being</u> with them. She enjoys <u>spending</u> the holidays with all her family. Other people like <u>being</u> in a small family. I am an only child. I like <u>spending</u> time alone, but I also enjoy <u>spending</u> time with my friend's large family. Overall, I prefer my small family, but I like <u>having</u> lots of friends!

Exercise 2.11 (page 24)

1. b   2. c   3. a   4. a   5. c

Exercise 2.12 (page 25)

Answers will vary.

Exercise 2.13 (page 26)

2. i   3. I   4. i   5. i   6. I   7. I   8. I

Exercise 2.14 (page 26)

2. a   3. a   4. a   5. b

Exercise 2.15 (page 27)

Answers will vary.

Spelling Skills (page 28)

1. grandmother   2. swimming   3. video   4. weight   5. hobby

Unit 3: Describing People

Exercise 3.1 (page 30)

1. Canadian   2. India   3. Europe   4. Mexican   5. Asia

Exercise 3.2 (page 31)

1. b   2. b   3. c   4. c   5. c

Exercise 3.3 (page 32)

Answers will vary.

Exercise 3.4 (page 33)

1. angry   2. confused   3. lively   4. impatient / worried   5. relieved / tired

Exercise 3.5 (page 33)

1. enthusiastic   2. nervous   3. sad   4. confident   5. relieved

Exercise 3.6 (page 34)

Answers will vary.

Exercise 3.7 (page 36)

Professor Foote <u>is feeling</u> sick today, so he <u>is staying</u> at home. Today's class is canceled. However, a discussion <u>is happening</u> online. Please go to the class website, and write your opinion about today's readings.

1. b   2. b   3. a   4. c

Exercise 3.8 (page 37)

2. is wearing   3. like   4. is moving   5. is talking

Exercise 3.9 (pages 37–38)

1. b   2. a   3. c   4. b   5. a   6. a

Exercise 3.10 (page 38)

Answers will vary.

Exercise 3.11 (page 39)

Is there a Loch Ness Monster? <u>No one</u> knows the answer to this question. There is <u>not any</u> evidence for the monster, but this does <u>not</u> mean that there is <u>nothing</u> in the lake. There are many attempts every year to find the monster, but <u>none</u> is ever successful. Is the monster hiding? Or is it just a legend? We may <u>never</u> know for certain.

Exercise 3.12 (page 39)

1. false   2. false   3. true   4. false   5. true

Exercise 3.13 (page 40)

Answers will vary. Sample responses:

2. School uniforms are not a good idea. Students don't have any choice. Uniforms are not cheap.

3. Children do not need cell phones. They do not help their education.

4. Some music is not relaxing. People feel angry or excited.

5. Vocabulary tests are not useful. Students don't learn anything. They don't like English classes with many tests.

Exercise 3.14 (page 41)

1. æ   2. ay   3. æ   4. ay   5. æ   6. ay   7. ay   8. æ   9. ay   10. ay

Exercise 3.15 (page 42)

1. describe   2. China   3. Canada   4. math   5. writing   6. languages
7. lively   8. online

Spelling Skills (page 43)

2. tired   3. nervous   4. lively   4. worried

Unit 4: Describing Places

Exercise 4.1 (page 45)

2. Student Union   3. Dormitory   4. Classrooms   5. Registrar   6. Library
7. Bookstore   8. Science Lab

Exercise 4.2 (page 46)

1. b   2. a   3. b   4. a   5. a

Exercise 4.3 (page 47)

1. dates   2. geography   3. experiments   4. business   5. poems

Exercise 4.4 (page 48)

Answers will vary.

Exercise 4.5 (pages 49–50)

1. Northside Apartments: a, c Central Apartments: d, e

2. b   3. c   4. a   5. b

Exercise 4.6 (page 50)

Answers will vary.

Exercise 4.7 (page 52)

1. behind   2. above   3. beside   4. outside   5. from

Exercise 4.8 (page 53)

1. d   2. a   3. e   4. b   5. c

Exercise 4.9 (page 55)

2. When you reach the student union, turn left.

3. I eat in my room if/when the cafeteria is closed.

4. If you like to study in a quiet place, I recommend the library.

5. If/When you live in a small town, you meet a lot of people.

Exercise 4.10 (page 56)

1. c   2. b   3. a   4. b   5. c

Exercise 4.11 (page 57)

Answers will vary.

Exercise 4.12 (page 57)

Answers will vary.

Spelling Skills (page 58)

1. science lab   2. visitor center   3. shopping mall   4. post office
5. public transportation

Unit 5: Describing Your Experiences

Exercise 5.1 (page 60)

move: walk, run, arrive, leave

talk: chat, argue, discuss, interrupt

see: notice, observe

Exercise 5.2 (page 61)

1. a. sit   b. prepare   c. contain   d. complete   e. take   f. appear
   g. write

2. Answers will vary.

Exercise 5.3 (page 62)

1. schedule   2. quiz   3. seminar   4. review   5. lab   6. presentation
7. unit

Exercise 5.4 (page 63)

1. c   2. a   3. e   4. b   5. d

2. a. false   b. true   c. true   d. false   e. true   f. false

3. Answers will vary. Sample response:

> The student chooses a business major and a computer science minor. He likes both subjects, and he has good grades. He wants to work for a technology company, so he wants to study computer science and business. The university has a minor in computer science but not in business.

Exercise 5.5 (page 66)

2. learned   3. watched   4. listened   5. helped   6. typed

Exercise 5.6 (page 66)

Answers will vary.

Exercise 5.7 (pages 67–68)

1. b   2. a   3. b   4. c   5. Travel agents: a, d, g

Travel websites: b, e

Exercise 5.8 (page 69)

Answers will vary.

Exercise 5.9 (page 70)

2. taught   3. gave   4. wrote   5. did   6. got   7. felt

Exercise 5.10 (page 71)

Corrected paragraph:

When I <u>was</u> in elementary school, we <u>had</u> a uniform. We <u>wore</u> gray shorts, a white shirt, and black shoes. I hated it! We all <u>found</u> ways to break the rules. For example, one of my friends always had brown shoes, not black. The teachers <u>were</u> always angry with us. However, another of my friends <u>went</u> to a school with no uniform. The students chose their own clothes. They <u>did</u> not break the rules, and they were much happier than us. Therefore, uniforms are bad for discipline.

Exercise 5.11 (page 72)

1. / t /   2. / d /   3. / d /   4. / ɪd /   5. / d /

Exercise 5.12 (page 73)

Answers will vary.

Spelling Skills (page 74)

1. biology   2. business   3. appear   4. receive   5. type

Unit 6: Giving Reasons

Exercise 6.1 (page 76)

Answers will vary. Sample responses:
1. enjoy / like   2. dislike / don't care for   3. hates / loves   4. fun / boring
5. awesome / awful

Exercise 6.2 (page 77)

1. b   2. c   3. c   4. b   5. a

Exercise 6.3 (page 78)

Answers will vary.

Exercise 6.4 (page 79)

	Where does it take place?	What does the student want?	Can the other person help? (Yes or no)
2	library	check out books	Yes
3	cashier's office	pay by credit card	No
4	advisor / professor's office	choose classes	Yes
5	front desk	apply to graduate school	Yes

Exercise 6.5 (page 80)

1. c   2. a   3. e   4. d   5. b

Exercise 6.6 (page 80)

1. b   2. a   3. c   4. a   5. c

Exercise 6.7 (page 81)

Answers will vary.

Exercise 6.8 (page 84)

1. a   2. b   3. b   4. a   5. c

Exercise 6.9 (page 84)

Answers may vary. Sample responses:
2. Where is the park?
3. Why do you like classical music?
4. Do you eat here often?
5. You like your roommate, don't you?

Exercise 6.10 (page 85)

1. b   2. c   3. b   4. a   5. c   6. a

Exercise 6.11 (page 87–88)

Madame Butterfly is one of the most popular operas today, (but) it was not popular at its first performance in 1904. At that time, people cheered during an opera (because) they liked it, (but) no one cheered for *Madame Butterfly*. In fact, the audience hated the opera, (so) they shouted bad things at the singers and the writer. (Because) the first audience did not enjoy *Madame Butterfly*, it closed after that performance. Later, audiences loved the opera, (and) now there are many performances of the opera every year.

1. c   2. a   3. c   4. a   5. c

Exercise 6.12 (page 88)

1. and   2. or   3. but   4. so   5. because

Exercise 6.13 (page 89)

1. / č /   2. / ž /   3. / š /   4. / ǰ /   5. / č /   6. / š /   7. / ž /   8. / č /
9. / ǰ /   10. / š /

Exercise 6.14 (page 90)

Do you enjoy wa<u>tch</u>ing televi<u>si</u>on? Why, or why not?

I don't wa<u>tch</u> televi<u>si</u>on any more. I just wa<u>tch</u> my favorite <u>sh</u>ows online. I enjoy wa<u>tch</u>ing videos on the Internet because I <u>ch</u>oose the time to wa<u>tch</u> them. I u<u>s</u>ually tune in late at night to ca<u>tch</u> up. And I wa<u>tch</u> <u>sh</u>ows from different places: A<u>s</u>ia, <u>G</u>ermany, or Brazil. I get more informa<u>ti</u>on, and I see almost no commer<u>ci</u>als.

Spelling Skills (page 91)

1. cash   2. exciting   3. energy   4. return   5. apply

Unit 7: Giving Opinions

Exercise 7.1 (pages 93–94)

1. <u>In my opinion</u>, blogs are a <u>great</u> idea, especially for college students. <u>I believe that</u> college students have to learn to think for themselves. Blogs are <u>important</u> because you can write your opinion in them. Other people can give feedback, and this is <u>essential</u> because you discover if other people agree with you. Blogs are <u>better</u> than diaries, <u>in my opinion</u>. Diaries are <u>old-fashioned</u>. They are private, but young people want to express themselves in public. Overall, <u>I think</u> blogs are <u>really cool</u>!

2. Answers may vary. Sample responses:

   a. Good

   b. College students

   c. i. You can write your opinion. ii. You can receive feedback.

   d. Diaries

   e. You can't express yourself in public.

   f. Overall

3. Answers will vary.

Exercise 7.2 (page 95)

1. 1. Bad   2. Good   3. Good   4. Bad   5. Bad

2. Student 1: No way, terrible; I don't agree.
   Student 2: I think, good
   Student 3: Yes, I do!, in my opinion
   Student 4: better

Exercise 7.3 (page 96)

2. e   3. a   4. d   5. g   6. b   7. f   8. c   9. h

Exercise 7.4 (pages 97–98)

1. a   2. b   3. c   4. c   5. a   6. c

Exercise 7.5 (page 98)

1. a   2. b   3. a   4. b   5. b

Exercise 7.6 (page 101)

1. smaller   2. more interesting   3. more useful   4. more slowly   5. more books

Exercise 7.7 (pages 101–2)

1. c   2. b   3. b   4. c   5. a   6. c

Exercise 7.8 (page 103)

Answers will vary.

Exercise 7.9 (page 104)

Answers may vary. Sample responses:

2. Members of a group have to work together.

3. People can make mistakes.

4. A group of people could consider many ideas.

5. A group should make better decisions than individuals.

Exercise 7.10 (pages 104–5)

1. c   2. a   3. c   4. b   5. a   6. c

Exercise 7.11 (page 105)

Answers will vary.

Exercise 7.12 (page 106)

1. opinion   2. ridiculous   3. important   4. dormitory   5. decision

6. university   7. building   8. conversation   9. expensive   10. absolutely

Exercise 7.13 (page 107)

   1. Answers may vary. Sample responses:
      a. One of the group members is not cooperating.
      b. i. Discuss the problem with the professor.   ii. Give the groupmate a part of the
          project to do by himself.

   2. a. eco<u>nom</u>ics   b. p<u>ro</u>ject   c. p<u>rob</u>lem   d. co<u>op</u>erate   e. to<u>get</u>her
      f. <u>grou</u>pmate   g. con<u>nec</u>t   h. so<u>lu</u>tion

   3. Answers will vary.

Spelling Skills (page 108)

1. opinion   2. unfortunately   3. project   4. absolutely   5. cooperate

Unit 8: Summarizing

Exercise 8.1 (page 110)

Answers may vary. Sample responses:
1. first   2. In addition   3. Finally

Exercise 8.2 (page 111)

   1. a. hurricane   b. cyclone   c. tropical storm

   2. c

   3. Answers will vary. Sample response:

      The lecture describes three kinds of storms. A tropical storm has low wind

      speeds. There are two kinds of severe storm. First, hurricanes form over the

      North Atlantic Ocean and have a category from 1 to 5. Second, cyclones are

      storms in the Pacific Ocean.

Exercise 8.3 (pages 112–13)

   1. c   2. c   3. b   4. a   5. c

Exercise 8.4 (pages 114–15)

1. a, c, d, e, g, h

2. Answers will vary.

3. Answers will vary. Sample responses:
   a. a third option called an Early College high school
   b. there is no tuition for Early College courses
   c. students in the Early College finish a community college degree before they finish high school

Exercise 8.5 (page 117)

Answers will vary. Sample responses:

1. the lowest   2. The most important   3. the most useful   4. the best

5. the happiest

Exercise 8.6 (page 117)

1. the most first problem → the first problem

2. the most big difficulty → the biggest difficulty

3. The goodest → The best

4. the more important → the most important

Exercise 8.7 (page 118)

Answers will vary.

Exercise 8.8 (page 119)

1. the cafeteria   2. The lecture   3. problems   4. an apple   5. a good idea

Exercise 8.9 (page 119)

1. The   2. a . . . The   3. the   4. Ø   5. The . . . a

Exercise 8.10 (page 120)

1. b   2. a   3. b   4. b   5. a

Exercise 8.11 (page 121)

1. the   2. the   3. a   4. an   5. a   6. the

Exercise 8.12 (page 122)

Answers may vary. This is the stress pattern on the CD.

The conversation is about the woman's <u>roommate</u>. She wants a <u>different</u> roommate. The man suggests talking to the <u>housing</u> office. However, <u>she</u> wants to talk directly to her roommate. The <u>best</u> solution is talking to her roommate. I think she should be <u>honest</u>. She wants to be <u>friends</u> with her roommate. So, they have to <u>agree</u>. I think the roommate might <u>want</u> to move. Then, they'll <u>both</u> be happier.

Exercise 8.13 (pages 122–23)

1. Answers may vary. Sample responses:

What does the child eat?	No nuts before 2 years old.	Small, increasing amounts of nuts
Good result	Cannot get sick	May be able to eat nuts
Problem	May never eat nuts	May get sick

2. Answers will vary.

Spelling Skills (page 123)

1. competitive   2. earn   3. However   4. First   5. finally

Audio Transcripts

Unit 1: Stepping Up to the iBT

Exercise 1.3 (page 4). (Track 2)

1.	*Professor:*	OK, everyone. Please begin the reading section of the test.
2.	*Student 1:*	Hey, Annie.
	Student 2:	Hi, Mark. How are you doing?
	S1:	Not so good. I have a math test today.
3.	*Professor:*	For this task, you will read a passage and listen to a lecture. Then, you will write a summary of the essential information.
4.	*Speaker:*	Listen to the passage. Then, listen again before you answer the questions.
5.	*Student:*	Excuse me, Professor.
	Professor:	Yes, James.
	S:	Can we take notes during the listening section?
	P:	Yes, but don't write on the test paper.

Exercise 1.6 (page 7). (Track 3)

Professor: There are two sections on today's test: grammar and writing. Complete the grammar section first. Answer all the questions. Choose only one answer choice for each question. Then, start the writing section. Choose one question only. Give specific details and examples. You have 45 minutes. Good luck!

Exercise 1.12 (page 12). (Track 5)

I always study the directions for the test first. Then, I mainly review my notes and write practice essays. I ask my teacher to explain difficult points. I also like describing the test to a friend. If I can do that, I'm sure I understand everything!

Unit 2: Talking about Yourself

Exercise 2.2 (page 16). (Track 6)

Student: Good afternoon, Professor Grimes. I'm Julie. I'm in your English class.

Professor: Hello, Julie. You look familiar. Is this your first class with me?

S: Yes, but I think you know my brother, Frank.

P: Oh, right! How is he?

S: He's fine. He's married now.

P: So, do you have nephews or nieces?

S: Yes, Frank has a son, so I have one nephew.

P: That's great! Well, I'm pleased to have you in my class.

Exercise 2.8 (page 22). (Track 7)

Professor: The topic of today's lecture is physical education in schools. Schools sometimes stop physical education classes to save money, but this is a bad choice for their students' future. Sports are important for children. Playing sports is good for your health. It builds personal and team skills. Without sports, children put on too much weight. So, children need a hobby—a physical hobby like running, or swimming, or playing soccer—to do in their free time. Playing sports is fun and important. Now, please open your textbooks to page 157. . .

Exercise 2.9 (page 23). (Track 8)

1. The topic of today's lecture is physical education in schools.

2. Schools sometimes stop physical education classes to save money.

3. Sports are important for children.

4. Children need a hobby.

Exercise 2.11 (page 24). (Track 9)

Some people prefer having a large family. For example, my friend has five siblings. She loves being with them. She enjoys spending the holidays with all her family. Other people like being in a small family. I am an only child. I like spending time alone, but I also enjoy spending time with my friend's large family. Overall, I prefer my small family, but I like having lots of friends!

Unit 3: Describing People

Exercise 3.1 (page 30). (Track 12)

1. *Student 1:*   Hi, I'm Michael.

   Student 2:   Hi, Michael. I'm Jess. Where are you from?

   S1:   I'm from Canada.

2. *Student 1:*   So, what do you think of our new teacher?

   Student 2:   He's got an interesting accent. Where's he from?

   S1:   He's Mexican, I think.

3. *Professor:*   Many Europeans came to America in the nineteenth century. . . .

4. *Student 1:*   I like your shirt.

   Student 2:   Thanks. I got it in Mexico.

5. *Professor:*   Today is the lunar new year in many Asian countries.

Exercise 3.5 (page 33). (Track 13)

1. *Student:*   You got a great score on the test! That's really great news! Well done!

2. *Student:*   Excuse me, um, Professor? Um, can I ask you a question? I'm sorry, but, um, my essay is late. Can I give it to you tomorrow?

3. *Student:*   My cat died yesterday. Poor Whiskers.

4. *Student:*   Good afternoon, everyone. My name is Susan, and I'm going to talk to you today about city planning. First …

5. *Professor:*   Where are my keys? Oh, there they are. Whew!

Exercise 3.9 (pages 37–38). (Track 14)

Teaching Assistant: Hi, Max. How can I help you?

Student: Lisa, thanks for staying after class. I'm feeling really worried about the course.

TA:	Why? You're getting a good grade.
S:	Yeah, I know. But I don't think I can finish the paper for next week.
TA:	Why not?
S:	I'm taking five classes, and I have three papers due on the same day.
TA:	That often happens! So, how can I help you?
S:	I am writing the paper for your class now, but I'm not going to finish in time. Can I turn it in on Friday instead of Wednesday?
TA:	I don't make that decision. I'll ask Professor King, and I'll tell you tomorrow.
S:	OK. Thanks.

Exercise 3.12 (page 39). (Track 15)

Professor:	OK, everyone. Today, we are talking about electric cars. Currently, there are few electric cars available to the general public. The problem is the battery: the batteries don't work for a long time. No one wants a car that can only go a few miles. But companies are working on better batteries. Electric cars are attractive because they use no gas, so there isn't any air pollution. Yes, David?
Student:	Professor, isn't there any pollution from making the electricity?
P:	Good point! That's true. There is no completely clean electricity now—maybe some day. But electric cars are much better for the environment than regular cars.

Exercise 3.15 (page 42). (Track 17)

I am going to describe my friend Jack. He is from Hong Kong in China. He is not like me. I am from Canada, and I am studying math. Jack loves writing. He is taking classes in languages and literature. Jack is always happy and lively. He's living at home and taking classes online this semester, so we aren't hanging out as much as usual these days.

Unit 4: Describing Places

Exercise 4.2 (page 46). (Track 18)

Assistant:	Good morning. Can I help you?
Parent:	Yes, I'm visiting my son, but I can't remember where we're meeting. I know it was a public building.
A:	Perhaps the student union? A lot of students go there to study. And it has a nice coffee shop.
P:	No, I don't think so. We're going to have lunch together.
A:	There are three cafeterias on campus. One is in the dormitory building. The second is near the library. And the third cafeteria is near the main classroom building, Angell Hall.
P:	Oh, I think we're meeting in the cafeteria by the library. Where is the library?
A:	Go outside the visitor's center, and turn left. The library is the tall building.
P:	Thanks. One more question: Do you sell t-shirts with the university's logo here?
A:	No, but you can buy them at the bookstore.
P:	Thanks for your help.
A:	No problem. Enjoy your visit!

Exercise 4.5 (pages 49–50). (Track 19)

Student:	Hi, I'm looking for an apartment for next year. Can you help me?
Housing Officer:	Of course. Where would you like to live?
S:	I want to be downtown with access to shops.
H:	Then, what about Northside Apartments? They're close to the shopping mall.
S:	Mall? Does it have a large parking lot?
H:	Yes.
S:	Oh, I don't want to live near a lot of traffic.
H:	OK. We also have Central Apartments. They're near the park and the lake.

S:	That sounds nice. I like jogging. Is it convenient for public transportation?
H:	Very. It's close to the bus station.
S:	How much is the rent?
H:	$400 a month for a one-bedroom apartment or $700 for a two-bedroom apartment.
S:	I'd like the one-bedroom, please. When does the lease start?
H:	You can move in on July 1.

Exercise 4.10 (page 56). (Track 20)

| Professor: | Your final papers are due on Friday. If you finish your paper early, you can give it to me in Wednesday's class. If you don't give it to me on Wednesday, please bring it to my office. My office is in Brock Hall. When you go into the building, take the elevator to the third floor. When you get out of the elevator, turn left. My office is number 312. If my door is locked, you can slide your paper under the door. Any questions? |

Unit 5: Describing Your Experiences

Exercise 5.4 (page 63). (Track 22)

Advisor:	Hi, Martin. How can I help you today?
Student:	Uh, well, I read the notice about declaring a major.
A:	Uh-huh. And what is your major?
S:	I'm not sure yet. I can't decide between computer science and business. I really like both subjects.
A:	Well, let me take a look at your grades. [pause; papers shuffle] You have good grades in both computer science and business. What do you want to do after you graduate?
S:	Maybe get a job with a technology company. So, I have to study both subjects.
A:	I see. Well, you can only have one major. But here's an idea. We have a minor in computer science.
S:	What's a minor?

A:	It means that your major is business, but that you have studied a lot about computer science as well.
S:	That sounds good. Can I study for a minor in business?
A:	No, we don't have a minor in business.
S:	Well, that's an easy decision, then. So, my major is business, and my minor is computer science. Now, how do I register for classes?

Unit 6: Giving Reasons

Exercise 6.2 (page 77). (Track 24)

Professor:	So, Mandy, do you have a topic for your term paper yet?
Student:	Not really, Professor. Could you help me?
P:	Sure. What did you find interesting in the class?
S:	I didn't really like learning about cells. And I didn't like studying the human body. But I really liked the topic of nutrition. That was so interesting.
P:	OK. Well, why did you find it interesting?
S:	It's fascinating, you know? I enjoyed learning about how we turn food into energy. And you taught me that I am eating badly—it's awful! So, I now eat better. I even enjoy vegetables. I really disliked eating vegetables before I took your class.
P:	That's great! Can you use that idea for your term paper?
S:	Eating vegetables?
P:	Not exactly. I think that's a fairly dull topic. Remember that you need to ask a good question in your term paper. I prefer the idea of learning to eat better.
S:	Oh, I have an idea! How can we teach young people about nutrition?
P:	I think that's a great topic.
S:	Awesome! Thanks for your help, Professor.
P:	Good luck with your paper. It's due on the 29th.

Exercise 6.2, Question 3 (page 77). (Track 25)

Student:	I didn't really like learning about cells. And I didn't like studying the human body. But I really liked the topic of nutrition. That was so interesting.

Exercise 6.4 (page 79). (Track 26)

1. *Housing Officer:*   Can I help you?

    Student: Yes, I'd like to ask about my room assignment for next year.

    H: What's your question?

    S: Can I change my roommate?

    H: I'm sorry, but you have to wait until May. I can't do anything about it now.

2. *Student:*   I'd like to check out these books, please?

    Librarian: Certainly. Could I see your ID card, please? Thank you.

3. *Student:*   I have a question about my tuition bill.

    Cashier: Uhuh.

    S: It was due yesterday. Can I still pay by credit card today?

    C: I don't know. I'll have to ask my supervisor.

4. *Advisor:*   Hello, Mark. How are you today?

    Student: Not so good, Dr. Scott. I'm really worried about my classes for next semester. I don't know which courses to take next. Can you help me?

    A: Sure. You're a math major, right? Well, let's see about the courses for next semester . . .

5. *Secretary:*   Good morning.

    Student: Yes, good morning. I'm applying for graduate school here in the fall. How do I do that?

    Sec: Well, you need to fill out an application form, and then mail it to us.

Exercise 6.6 (page 80). (Track 27)

    Student: Hi, can you help me?

    Housing Officer: What's the problem?

    S: I'm not happy with my room assignment for next year.

    H: Really? Why not?

S:	My dorm room is so expensive. I don't think I can pay all that money. What can I do?
H:	Do you have a single room or a double for next year?
S:	A single.
H:	OK. In that case, I can move you to a double room. That will be a lot cheaper.
S:	Yeah, but I hate living with roommates. There are always so many problems, you know?
H:	Not always. I had great roommates in college. But if you don't want a roommate, your other option is to live off campus.
S:	You mean, find an apartment?
H:	Right. You can share a two-bedroom apartment. You have a private room, and you share the rent.
S:	That's a good idea. Let me think about it.

Exercise 6.6, Question 5 (page 80). (Track 28)

Housing Officer:	Right. You can share a two-bedroom apartment. You have a private room, and you share the rent.
Student:	That's a good idea. Let me think about it.

Exercise 6.8 (page 84). (Track 29)

1. Where is the bookstore?

2. How did you get here?

3. Did you go to Dr. Baker's lecture?

4. Excuse me. This is the housing office, isn't it?

5. Why do you enjoy playing golf?

Exercise 6.10 (page 85). (Track 30)

Professor:	So, how do credit card companies make money? They have three ways to make money. The first is interest—that's the money you pay to the credit card company because you are borrowing money from them to pay for your purchases.

Student 1:	But if you pay the full bill every month, you don't pay interest, do you?
P:	That's true: if you pay your bill, you don't pay interest. But a lot of other people don't pay the full bill, and they pay a lot of interest.
Student 2:	Does the credit card company make any other money from customers?
P:	Yes, they do. They charge fees.
S1:	What kind of fees do they charge?
P:	For example, some credit cards charge an annual fee. Others charge a fee if you pay your bill late. There are lots of fees on some cards. So that's two ways they make money. What about the third? Who else pays money to the credit card companies?
S2:	The store owner. My father owns a bookstore. He pays money to the credit card companies when a customer uses a card.
P:	Exactly. Bookstores, restaurants, travel agents, online shopping sites . . . they all pay money to the credit companies.
S2:	I didn't know that. But why don't they just stop taking credit cards? My father could save a lot of money!
P:	It's not that easy. 80 percent of Americans have a credit card, and many people want to pay with them. If you don't take credit cards, you lose customers.

Exercise 6.14 (page 90). (Track 32)

I don't watch television any more. I just watch my favorite shows online. I enjoy watching videos on the Internet because I choose the time to watch them. I usually tune in late at night to catch up. And I watch shows from different places: Asia, Germany, or Brazil. I get more information, and I see almost no commercials.

Unit 7: Giving Opinions

Exercise 7.2 (page 95). (Track 33)

Listen to different students answer the question: Do you think the legal driving age should be increased to 18 years old?

Student 1:	No way! That's a terrible idea!
Student 2:	Yeah, I think that's good. A lot of younger drivers are in car accidents.
Student 3:	Yes, I do! My brother is 16, and in my opinion, he's too young to drive.
Student 4:	I don't know. 18 seems kind of old. 17 is better.
Student 1:	I don't think so. Teenagers need to drive in high school so their parents don't have to drive them everywhere.

Exercise 7.4 (pages 97–98). (Track 34)

Student:	Can I talk to you for a minute?
Teaching Assistant:	Sure, Tim. What can I do for you?
S:	Well, it's about the last quiz.
TA:	Uhuh.
S:	I got a really bad grade.
TA:	Yes, I know. What happened?
S:	Well, you know I am on the school tennis team. We had a very important match the day before the quiz, and I guess I was just too tired in class. I absolutely have to pass this class. What can I do?
TA:	Maybe you can do an extra-credit assignment. Then you can show that you completely understand the content of the course.
S:	Really? That would be awesome.
TA:	OK, but unfortunately, I can't make the decision. I have to talk to Professor Warner.
S:	Do you think he'll agree?
TA:	Probably. He's usually quite flexible.
S:	Really? He always seems so strict.

TA:	Yeah, but actually he just wants to know that you are serious about the class. I'll write to him, but you should probably also send him an email.
S:	Absolutely! I'll do that right now.
TA:	OK. Well, good luck.
S:	Thanks!

Exercise 7.4, Question 3 (page 97). (Track 35)

Student:	I absolutely have to pass this class. What can I do?
Teaching Assistant:	Maybe you can do an extra-credit assignment. Then you can show that you completely understand the content of the course.
S:	Really? That would be awesome.
TA:	OK, but unfortunately, I can't make the decision. I have to talk to Professor Warner.

Exercise 7.10 (pages 104–5). (Track 36)

Student 1:	Did you choose your room for next year, Dana?
Student 2:	No. Do we have to do that now?
S1:	Absolutely! You have to choose your room assignment this week.
S2:	Oh, no! I had no idea. Which dorm building should I choose?
S1:	Well, you can choose between the River Building and the Smith Building.
S2:	Can I live in the Jones Street dorms?
S1:	No. They're already full.
S2:	I don't like the Smith dorms. They're older than the others.
S1:	I agree. The River Building is nicer.
S2:	Right, I should apply for the River Building. What do I have to do now?
S1:	You need to find a roommate.
S2:	OK.
S1:	Then, you have to fill in a form. You must go to the housing office to do that.
S2:	Thanks!

Exercise 7.13 (page 107). (Track 38)

Student 1:   Hi, Lee. How's your economics project going?

Student 2:   Not so good. I have a problem with one of the people in my group.

S1:   Really?

S2:   Yeah. He wants to work by himself. He won't cooperate. But we have to work together. What can I do?

S1:   Can you discuss the problem with your professor? She could talk to this guy.

S2:   Maybe. But she wants us to solve our problems ourselves.

S1:   Huh. Is there part of the project that your groupmate can do by himself? And you can connect the parts of the project at the end.

S2:   That could be a good solution. But it won't be easy.

Unit 8: Summarizing

Exercise 8.2 (page 111). (Track 39)

Professor: Today, I'm going to talk about severe weather systems called cyclones and hurricanes. Both of these weather systems are organizations of thunderstorms and clouds in a circular pattern. Circular means that from above, they look like very big circles, OK? If the storm is in the North Atlantic Ocean, it's called a hurricane. We give hurricanes a category from 1 to 5—a number that describes its strength, including wind speed. A Category 5 hurricane is the strongest, has the highest wind speed. In the Pacific Ocean, near Asia, for example, hurricanes are called cyclones. There's actually a third kind of storm that I should mention. If the wind speed is not high enough to be a Category 1 hurricane or cyclone, we call it a tropical storm.

Exercise 8.4 (pages 114–15). (Track 40)

Professor: One of the biggest problems in higher education today is improving access. By access, I mean the ability of students to go to college, especially students who traditionally do not go to a college or university. Community colleges are cheaper than universities, but they are still too expensive for many students. In addition, some high school students think that any college is too hard or too slow; they want to get a job and earn money. So, one new solution is the Early College High School. If you go to an Early College High School, you take community college classes during your years at high school. When you finish high school, you already have a community college degree. Or, you can apply those classes to a university program, so you only have to study for two more years after high school to get a university degree. I think this is a really exciting idea. Any questions so far?

Exercise 8.10 (page 120). (Track 41)

Student:	Dr. Stokes, can I ask you a question?
Professor:	Sure, Scott. What is it?
S:	I'm choosing classes for next semester.
P:	Uhuh.
S:	I want to take your art class.
P:	Great!
S:	But, I have a problem with the schedule. I have a physics class at 10 AM right before your art class in a different building. I might be a bit late for your class.
P:	That's not good. You really have to be on time.
S:	What can I do?
P:	Mine is the only art class next semester. Can you change your physics class? Are there other sections of the class?
S:	Yes, there are a lot of sections, but only two are still open. There's an 8 AM section. But that's so early!
P:	Well, I think you have a choice. If you want to take my art class, you must take the 8 AM physics class.
S:	OK, I'll do that. Thank you, Professor.
P:	See you next semester.

Exercise 8.10, Question 4 (page 120). (Track 42)

Professor:	Mine is the only art class next semester. Can you change your physics class? Are there other sections of the class?

Student: Yes, there are a lot of sections, but only two are still open. There's an 8 AM section. But that's so early!

Exercise 8.11 (Page 121). (Track 43)

P: Mine is the only art class next semester. Can you change your physics class? Are there other sections of the class?

S: Yes, there are a lot of sections, but only two are still open. There's an 8 AM section. But that's so early!

P: Well, I think you have a choice. If you want to take my art class, you must take the 8 AM physics class.

Exercise 8.12 (Page 122). (Track 44)

Student: The conversation is about the woman's roommate. She wants a different roommate. The man suggests talking to the housing office. However, she wants to talk directly to her roommate. The best solution is talking to her roommate. I think she should be honest. She wants to be friends with her roommate. So, they have to agree. I think the roommate might want to move. Then, they'll both be happier.

Exercise 8.13 (pages 122–23). (Track 45)

Professor: There are two different opinions about treating children with nut allergies. If a child might have a nut allergy—for example because his parents have it—most doctors say the child must not eat any nuts until at least two years of age. If the child doesn't eat any nuts, he won't have an allergy and get sick. But he may never eat nuts even when he grows up. However, some doctors disagree. They give small amounts of nuts to young children. They slowly increase the amount of nuts. They find that some of these children don't get the allergy, and they can eat nuts and not get sick. But other children who try this treatment can get sick. In fact, they can develop a very serious allergy. So, is it worth the risk? Each parent and doctor has to make that decision.

Appendix A (page 124). (Track 46)